THE SHROPPIE

A portrait of the Shropshire Union main line
and its Middlewich branch

Thomas Pellow and Paul Bowen

The Landscape Press
in association with The Boat Museum

ISBN 0 947849 00 9

Distributed by
The Boat Museum, Dockyard Road, Ellesmere Port, South Wirral. L65 4EF

Printed by Johnsons of Nantwich Limited

CONTENTS

The front cover painting by Alan Firth shows "Gifford" – an ex Thomas Clayton tar boat – in her horse-drawn working days. She made regular trips on the Shropshire Union, carrying oil from Stanlow on the Manchester Ship Canal down to Oldbury in the Midlands. When Clayton's gave up canal carrying in 1966 "Gifford" was bought privately, eventually restored and is now preserved at The Boat Museum, Ellesmere Port.

Edwardian High Summer. The "Shroppie" in its heyday. Two fully laden boats, both belonging to the Shropshire Union Railways and Canal Company pass below Holling's Bridge (No. 58) in the cutting to the south of Market Drayton in 1911.

Tow path, cutting and canal banks are all in excellent condition – and as befits a canal controlled by a railway company the route is also in use for telephone and telegraph wires.

I : BEGINNINGS : 1772-1835

Exploring the main line of the Shropshire Union canal leaves two strong impressions.

Above all else it is rural. The sixty-six mile route of the waterway lies sandwiched between two industrial centres — but despite this it is predominantly a country canal. At the north end is Ellesmere Port and the industrial sprawl along the banks of the River Mersey. To the south are the fringes of the Black Country and the edge of Wolverhampton. But between these two centres the canal slips quietly along as if trying to avoid towns wherever possible. The wide vistas of the Cheshire Plain are interrupted only by the cathedral city of Chester and the margins of the half-timbered town of Nantwich. The wooded cuttings and high embankments of the Shropshire section avoid urban areas almost entirely. The canal skirts round the edge of the quiet country town of Market Drayton and passes within reach of only a handful of large villages. For the rest it is in countryside.

The other impression of the Shropshire Union is one of unity. Here is a canal that seems all of a piece, a link between the sprawling canal system of the industrialised Midlands at one end — and the industrial north west with access to the sea at the other.

However, it was neither the intention of its builders to create a canal idyll — nor originally to even follow the present day route. Its earliest origins lie back in the early days of the canal era — and in Cheshire rather than Shropshire! To further complicate matters three separate companies were involved in its building and to two different widths — the final stage of the main line being the last major narrow boat canal ever to be built.

By the early 1770's the business community of Chester was beginning to feel itself at risk. Their county town was a river port, the Dee navigation allowing boats to come up-stream from the North Wales coast and the Irish Sea. No real rival to their trade existed until in 1766 when — partly at the instigation of Josiah Wedgewood who was concerned to improve the transport of both china clay and finished pottery — an Act of Parliament was passed authorising the construction of a canal to connect the rivers Trent and Mersey. This "Grand Trunk Canal" connecting the Potteries with Hull and Liverpool would boost the Merseyside port at the expense of Chester.

The local businessmen of Chester therefore promoted their own canal to connect with the Trent and Mersey at Middlewich. This was in the hope that goods such as salt and pottery would then be exported from Chester instead of being carried via the Rivers Weaver and Mersey to Liverpool and beyond.

Not surprisingly the Duke of Bridgewater, with his associates of the Trent and Mersey Canal Company, objected to a junction with the Chester Canal on commercial grounds; a classic case of parochial canal protectionism. They feared that the new canal would draw traffic away from the northern section of the Trent and Mersey. As a consequence of this opposition, the

Chester Canal Act of 1772 – to the dismay of its Cheshire promoters-included a harsh clause which prohibited it from coming within one hundred yards of the Trent and Mersey!

This was a major blow to the Chester Canal Company and it led to a hasty revision of their original plans. They decided that their main line should instead run from Chester to Nantwich with only a branch to Middlewich. However, it was to be over sixty years before this branch was actually built.

Construction of the canal commenced in Chester during 1772 but progress was slow owing to a combination of engineering and financial problems. These held up completion until 1779. No less than £71,000 was spent on building the canal to Nantwich, a massive burden for a small local Company whose potential traffic was clearly limited.

Initially strenuous efforts were made to attract business; some passenger boats were laid on and there were attempts to generate the carriage of goods such as rock salt, but this did not materialize. The financial position of the canal quickly deteriorated and it received a further blow in November 1787 when a lock at Beeston collapsed. In 1792 Phillips 'Inland Navigation' commented that the Chester Canal "is likely to be productive of great advantage to the county of Chester and also to the country through which it passes". But this optimism proved completely unfounded for as Charles Hadfield has pointed out in *"The Canals of the West Midlands"*, "This project was the first thoroughly unsuccessful canal"......so unsuccessful was the canal that it became semi-derelict.

But in 1791 the gloom and despondency of the Chester Canal Committee was partially lifted by the deliberations of businessmen in the neighbouring county of Shropshire.

On 31st. August 1791 a meeting was held in the inland town, Ellesmere, to discuss the building of a grandiose network of canals linking the Rivers Severn, Dee and Mersey. It was proposed to construct a canal from the then small fishing village of Netherpool on the Mersey, across the Wirral Peninsula to Chester. From there the canal was to swing westwards to tap the coal and iron producing district of north east Wales before resuming it's rural progress southwards through Ellesmere, and eventually on to Shrewsbury and the River Severn.

The Ellesmere Canal was born at the height of the Canal Mania when fortunes were to be made from investments in this new transport system. September 10th. 1792 must have been one of the most remarkable days in Ellesmere's history as the small town was invaded by would-be investors frantically trying to place their subscriptions. The Company obtained its Act on April 30th. 1793. William Jessop was appointed engineer in overall charge, to be ably assisted by the then relatively unknown Thomas Telford.

Work on the Wirral Line, the first section of this planned Mersey to Severn canal began in November 1793. The first nine miles of canal from the River Mersey to Chester opened on July 1st. 1795. From the very start it was a successful enterprise. It carried a wide variety of goods and passengers

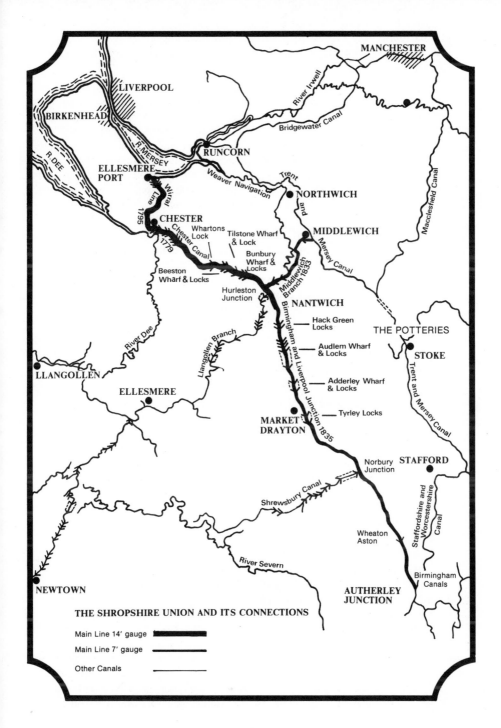

THE SHROPSHIRE UNION AND ITS CONNECTIONS

Main Line 14' gauge

Main Line 7' gauge

Other Canals

who patronised the express flyboats. The neighbouring villages of Netherpool and Whitby on the Mersey developed into an important canal terminus, Ellesmere Port, the port of the Ellesmere Canal.

The remainder of the Company's ambitious scheme did not reach fruition. High inflation during the Napoleonic Wars resulted in soaring building costs and capital became scarce as confidence faded. Telford's brilliant but expensive aqueducts at Chirk and Pontcysyllte on the Welsh sections had taken ten years to build and the Company's enthusiasm for a direct canal from Wales to Chester waned with the daunting prospect of taking it across further difficult terrain. They were forced to settle for a more local network than originally planned. This at least proved quite profitable, carrying miscellaneous local cargoes, such as iron, coal, slate, limestone and timber.

The planned route north of Pontcysyllte was abandoned, whilst in the south the canal petered out in fields half-way between Ellesmere and Shrewsbury. Gradually however, the Ellesmere Canal was pushed eastwards from Welsh Frankton to a junction with the Chester Canal at Hurleston, just north of Nantwich........but progress was remarkably slow due to the Company's pre-occupation with their ambitious aqueducts. The Chester Canal Company, irritated by the hesitancy of the Ellesmere to build a link between their two canals, threatened to cease supplying water to the Wirral section. This forced the Ellesmere Company into a specific agreement. Even so it was not until 1805 that the Chester Canal actually received its first cargo from the Ellesmere system.

By 1810 the Chester Canal's fortunes were improving, for it had assumed a position of strategic importance, sandwiched between the Ellesmere Company's two waterways. A merger was the most logical outcome and in 1813 the joint Ellesmere and Chester Canal Company came into existence. Under the auspices of this new regime efforts were directed towards boosting profitability. Low tolls on long distance cargoes were introduced in an attempt to encourage goods traffic and considerable investment was made in what was proving to be the popular passenger route from Chester to Liverpool. The old problem of subsidence and slippage in the sands along the canal at Beeston was seriously tackled, the installation of an iron lock by Telford providing the eventual solution.

The most striking weakness of the Ellesmere and Chester operation was the lack of a southern outlet to join up with the hub of the canal system in the West Midlands. What is now the northern half of the Shropshire Union main line was in effect an isolated group of canals that would only link rural Cheshire and parts of north east Wales with the sea. The joint company was no doubt greatly heartened therefore in 1824 when news broke of a scheme to link Nantwich with Autherley, a village on the northern outskirts of Wolverhampton. Isolation would be at an end. The prospect of this new canal also revived support for the Middlewich Branch. The Trent and Mersey company were still unenthusiastic about having a potential rival for their traffic — and especially one with links to the south, but the Ellesmere and Chester carried on undaunted and promoted a canal from Barbridge to the outskirts of Middlewich. From there the Trent and Mersey undertook to construct a short link to their own canal running through the other side of the town. By this time the railways were emerging as a potent threat to the viability of the canals — yet the Trent and Mersey still displayed a very narrow outlook by imposing heavy compensation tolls along their very short linking section. This was to make canal rates from Ellesmere Port to Middlewich quite uncompetitive for years to come.

Work began on the Middlewich Branch in July 1827 under the direction of Telford, who at the time was also consultant engineer for the Trent and Mersey. The branch was opened on 1st. September 1833, although it carried little traffic until the completion of the Birmingham and Liverpool two years later.

The Birmingham and Liverpool Junction Canal forms the southern half of what is now the Shropshire Union main line. It has been described as the "last victory of the canals over the railways". Almost as a final grand gesture it was built to coincide with what was to prove the beginnings of the "Railway Age". The genesis of the idea seems to have lain with Telford. In 1824 the Birmingham Canal Committee had directed him to suggest improvements to their own main line through the Black Country. By 1829 he had successfully straightened and shortened Brindley's originally winding Birmingham Canal. Telford's advice, however, did not stop there. He argued the need for a more efficient outlet for goods to the north than that provided by the winding and heavily locked Trent and Mersey. Telford's proposed canal would run northwards from the Black Country to create a direct link with the Mersey, then Britain's fastest growing export centre.

The need to compete with the growing threat of the railways also lay behind the canals promotion — because in the 1820's there was widespread talk of building a railway line from the Midlands to Liverpool. The waterways' interest for once united to forestall this commercial threat and the Birmingham Canal Company led the way in promoting the new navigation. On 22nd. September 1825 there was a subscription meeting at the Royal Victoria Hotel in Newport, Shropshire — a town roughly half-way between Nantwich and Wolverhampton. This was to raise money and support for the venture. In hindsight the canal's building came a generation too late. The public mood was moving in favour of the railways for high tolls and dividends had tarnished the image of the canal interest. Nevertheless the promoters were undeterred and in May 1826 an Act of Parliament was passed authorising the building of a canal from the Nantwich terminus of the Chester Canal to Autherley Junction. Here on the outskirts of Wolverhampton, the new canal would join with the Staffordshire and Worcestershire Canal. A year later another Act sanctioned a branch westwards from Norbury through Newport to the iron and coal fields of East Shropshire to link with the existing tub boat canals of that area.

BIRMINGHAM AND LIVERPOOL JUNCTION CANAL NAVIGATION.

Sir,

On the other side I have the honour to send you a Particular of the Proceedings at the last General Assembly of the Proprietors, held on the 30th of January last, with a Copy of the Notice issued for opening the Canal. I have also the honour to inclose a Copy of the Plan of the Canal, by which you will perceive that it may be considered as a continuation of the Birmingham Canal from Wolverhampton to the Ellesmere and Chester Canal, which passes on to the River Mersey at Ellesmere Port, having a Branch recently completed from the neighbourhood of Nantwich, into the Trent and Mersey Canal at Middlewich. A new and improved road is thus afforded for distribution of agricultural produce, and also for conveyance of manufactures from the Mineral Districts of Staffordshire and Worcestershire, and the towns of Birmingham and Wolverhampton, to the port of Liverpool and the town of Manchester, while by the junction also of this undertaking with the Shrewsbury Canal, the manufactures and produce of the county of Salop have very great advantages afforded for their more cheap and speedy conveyance to Liverpool, Manchester, Wolverhampton, the Mineral Districts of Staffordshire and Worcestershire, and the Metropolis.

I have the honour to be, Sir,

Your most obedient servant,

Clerk.

69, Newhall-street, Birmingham, Feb. 4, 1835.

The main line complete at last. The 1835 announcement of the opening of the Birmingham and Liverpool Junction – completing the route from Autherley Junction to Nantwich Basin.

The Birmingham and Liverpool was the last great narrowboat canal to be built and it is notable for Telford's brilliant and spectacular engineering. It has been described as "an exercise in virtuoso canal construction". Deep cuttings as at Woodseaves, and massive embankments, as at Shebdon, are the hallmarks of this waterway which ignores the contours so faithfully followed by the early canal builders. In doing so it anticipated the direct route building techniques later used by the railways.

Although construction commenced in 1826, through traffic was not able to use the navigation until 1835. This was primarily due to the constant slipping of the massive Shelmore embankment. The Birmingham and Liverpool Junction eventually cost some £800,000 to build − a huge sum for the time, and the Canal Committee had been forced to borrow so heavily that it was never able to pay a dividend.

The new canal was 39½ miles long and its 29 locks were purposely grouped, the majority being near Audlem. The passage time between Liverpool and Birmingham was reduced to 45 hours, while this missing link completed what we now know as the main line of the Shropshire Union Canal.

II : BUILDING THE CANAL

The construction of the Shropshire Union Main Line spanned a period of over sixty years.

Its central section, the Chester Canal, ranks among England's earliest 'cuts' but it was beset with problems right from the start when Joseph Taylor, the Mayor of Chester, cut the first sod in April 1772. The intended waterway was then regarded as an extension of the Dee Navigation and the sixteen locks on the route to Nantwich were built to broad canal dimensions — at just over 70 feet long and 13 feet wide being large enough to accommodate the river barges.

Whereas the contemporary and much grander Trent and Mersey Canal secured the services of the eminent James Brindley, the Chester Canal Committee employed a series of inexperienced engineers. The first to be engaged was a 'surveyor and contractor in cutting' called Samuel Weston but he was replaced in 1774 by Thomas Morris who had been involved in the building of the Bridgewater Canal. He lasted only a few months. A similar fate awaited his successor, Josiah Clowes, who was sacked for 'inattention to duty'. Other engineers duly followed before the canal was eventually finished — but this comical hiring and firing must have brought great displeasure to a dispirited Chester Canal Committee. The most difficult task confronting the builders was the making of a deep and wide cutting through solid sandstone rock beneath the city walls of Chester. An easier and cheaper line was unfortunately shunned by the engineers, although their job was made unexpectedly easier by the discovery of a Roman ditch along their line which proved comparatively easy to excavate. The progress of the Chester Canal was hindered by various problems. In 1774 a bridge was reported to have given way, whilst at Beeston the foundations of the lock were constantly being undermined by unstable running sand. The failure to complete the canal until 1779 reflected an amalgam of technical complications and severe cash shortages.

In contrast when the Ellesmere Company began cutting its canal across the Wirral Peninsula in November 1793, it was blessed with an engineering team of experience and talent. William Jessop of Newark supervised the whole scheme and he was already noted for his work on the Grand Canal in Ireland and also the Grand Junction Canal in England. Local men like John Duncombe of Oswestry and William Turner of Whitchurch were involved in surveying the route but their role was soon eclipsed by the rapidly rising Thomas Telford who was appointed 'General Agent, Surveyor, Engineer and Architect and Overlooker of the Works' on a salary of £300 per annum. This post was very demanding — for apart from supervising the day to day building, he had to organise payment of contractors and submit drawings of locks and buildings to Jessop for approval. Despite having been Shropshire's Surveyor of Public Works since 1787, nationally Telford was still a relatively unknown engineer. Although subsequent triumphs were to bring him fame, his work on the short Wirral Line was crucial in providing a valuable apprenticeship in canal engineering.

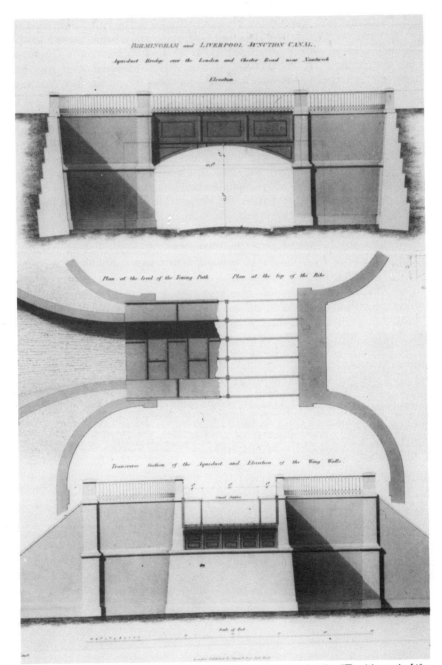

Telford's design for the aqueduct bridge just south of Nantwich as reproduced in "The Atlas to the Life of Thomas Telford by Himself" edited by J. Rickman and published in 1838. The aqueduct still remains as planned even down to the details of the railings.

13

Construction proved relatively straightforward. The Wirral line followed a level course through the Backford Gap, locks only being needed at the terminii. Samuel Weston, the Chester Canal's first engineer, was appointed the contractor — so his reputation must have recovered after his first unhappy experience with waterways. Progress was so smooth that the canal was open for traffic by July 1795.

Nevertheless this Wirral section proved expensive because, like the Chester, it was built to broad canal dimensions in order to carry the barges used on the Dee and Mersey estuaries. The large locks involved were costly both in terms of water as well as masonry. Fortunately the Chester Canal Committee agreed to supply the new canal with water but at Ellesmere Port a Boulton and Watt Steam pumping engine had to be installed at a cost of £1,576 to provide supplies from the Mersey. The engine was built by John Wilkinson of Bersham Ironworks near Wrexham — a leading member of the Ellesmere Canal Committee.

Between 1793 and 1805 the Ellesmere Company spent no less than £68,405 on its Wirral Line, an indication that canal building and maintenance was an expensive business.

The battle to construct the final section of the "Shroppie" — the Birmingham and Liverpool Junction Canal in the 1830's — provides one of the most heroic and fascinating stories in British waterway history. Thomas

A Shropshire Union Company horse boat – the "Dongola" about to enter Cowley Tunnel, near Gnosall, circa 1905. Typical of the construction difficulties on the southern section the tunnel had been planned as one of 700 yards – but owing to unexpected rock faults had to be opened out into this cutting – only 80 yards of tunnel remaining.

Telford was appointed principal engineer for this, the last great narrow boat canal. By this time he was well known for a number of mighty achievements — the Ellesmere, Caledonian and Gotha Canals, the Holyhead Road and the Menai Suspension Bridge. Despite the rumblings of the "Railway Mania" Telford refused to abandon his loyalty to the canal industry to the extent of turning down an offer of the post of engineer to the Liverpool and Manchester Railway. Ironically the line of his Canal closely followed the route of a proposed Birmingham to Liverpool Railway with which John Rennie and William Jessop, two other great canal builders, were involved.

Telford was determined to build an efficient waterway capable of competing with the railways. The adoption of an unusually direct route necessitated building massive earthworks with high embankments to cross valleys and making deep cuttings to slice through high ground — an approach that foretold the railway practice that was to follow. Responsibility for the building and execution of Telford's designs lay with Alexander Easton, who, as resident engineer, made his headquarters at Market Drayton.

The Birmingham and Liverpool was divided into three sections for contracting purposes. John Wilson, an experienced stonemason who had been with Telford since the great days of Pontcysyllte, was awarded the contract for the Nantwich to Tyrley length with a tender of £198,100. Work commenced in January 1827 and in a tour of inspection with Easton in July, Telford noted that Wilson's labour force of 1600 men was making 'smooth and rapid progress'. By January 1828 one third of the work had been finished on this length and Telford forecast completion in September. The movement of the large quantities of earth from the cuttings to the embankments was being achieved by boat. Once an easy stretch of canal had been cut it was made watertight with puddled clay and then was filled with water. This procedure was used by Wilson to build up the Tern embankment south of Market Drayton, the soil for which came from Adderley Leys cutting.

Towards the end of 1829 all the masonry had been finished apart from Audlem bottom lock. Building the "Shroppie" of course required many craftsmen as well as the unskilled navvies. The services of stonemasons, carpenters, bricklayers and blacksmiths were all essential in tasks like lock and bridge building. In the winter of 1829/1830 Wilson faced disaster when heavy rain caused the base of Nantwich Bank to move outwards under the weight of soil above, the flow of mud blocking the nearby Henhull Lane. A wet spring next hindered remedial work and by July 1830 three hundred yards of embankment south of the aqueduct had sunk several feet below the level of the canal. Fresh soil was brought in to stabilise the sliding mass but the problem was not completely mastered until 1832.

Whilst Wilson struggled in the north, the middle section, from Tyrley to Church Eaton, was also developing into a nightmare. In May 1829 this demanding contract was awarded to W.A. Provis, another of Telford's proteges from the Holyhead road. When work began in June the crumbling rock and clay of Woodseaves and Grub Street cuttings soon brought trouble. Retaining walls were built in an effort to shore up the rock faces but the winter rains and frosts dislodged masses of earth and rock. Even today such trouble is an ever present threat on these sections. Towards the end of that summer, 400 men and 70 horses set out to build up Shelmore Great Bank. Horse tramways were laid to bring spoil from the Grub Street and Cowley cuttings but progress was hindered by bad weather. In mid 1830 the northern end of Cowley Tunnel was tackled but the navvies soon broke into badly faulted rock which had to be shored up with timbering. After consultation Telford, Easton and Provis decided to open up the remainder of the tunnel as a cutting and of the proposed 690 yards only 81 remained as a tunnel. In his winter report of 1830 Telford noted that Shelmore had reached a quarter of its planned height but that subsidence was severe.

All the work on the canal was done without any mechanical aids. The navvies used a system of wheelbarrow runs to shift the soil after it had been excavated by pick and shovel. In deep cuttings horses would help to pull the barrows up the side of the cuttings. Many of the navvies employed on the Birmingham and Liverpool were, like the railway construction gangs who followed, noted for their hard work, rough living and excessive drinking. Needless to say the local inhabitants generally mistrusted and disliked them and in the Cheswardine area the navvies gained notoriety for their poaching and regular stealing of hens' eggs.

The third section of canal from Church Eaton to Autherley was again successfully tendered for by John Wilson. By July 1830 the route of the canal had already been marked out and drawings were made. Six hundred men and thirty five horses started work on this relatively easy section. But 1831 brought no easing of Telford's difficulties. In the north the Nantwich Bank was still shifting, whilst on January 9th. John Wilson died. The loss of Telford's trusted friend and right hand man for over 30 years was a great blow but fortunately Wilson's sons took charge and successfully completed the two contracts.

Telford's own health was now failing fast while the Canal Committee was increasingly alarmed by the engineering problems and the growing financial crisis they faced. The very real prospect of having two thousand unpaid labourers rioting in the Shropshire and Staffordshire countryside forced them to seek Government aid and the Exchequer Bill Loan Commissioners provided substantial loan facilities.

Nantwich Bank was finally conquered in 1832 — but Shelmore suffered disastrous collapses in August. The canal was effectively split into two useless parts. Telford's growing illness continued to handicap the enterprise. Easton noted in a letter to John Rickman that "on the evening of Saturday 8th September 1832 Telford arrived at the Corbet Arms Inn, Market Drayton in a poor state of health". As a desperate remedy Easton advocated the installation of a wooden trough for the canal along the Shelmore embankment so as to allow the canal to open.

The fortunes of the Birmingham and Liverpool reached their lowest point in 1833. The Canal Committee became openly critical of Telford's leadership and Charles Loch wrote to fellow committee member Lord Clive observing that "Telford is not the man he was". William Cubitt was appointed to deputise for Telford as Company engineer and so he met with the Canal Committee at the Royal Victoria Hotel, Newport for a tour of inspection. He ordered the sides of Woodseaves to be cut back and this hardcore to be dumped at Shelmore to consolidate the bank.

By the summer of 1833 the third section was at last nearing completion. Apart from the basic cutting of the canal there were numerous finishing tasks to be completed including gravelling the towpath, planting boundary hedges, erecting buildings, positioning milestones, planting trees and generally tidying up. In March 1834 a deaf and increasingly frail Telford made his last inspection of the canal. He had not been fit enough to view it for nearly two years. Although Shelmore was still shifting, "puddling" along this length was almost complete. The whole episode had embittered Telford who felt that had his original line not been forcibly altered, in order to protect Lord Anson's pheasants from disturbance in Shelmore Wood, the Great Bank which "caused so much trouble, expense and procrastination" would have been completely unnecessary.

In May, Shelmore collapsed once again — and Grub Street was blocked by a serious rock fall. Even Cubitt was by now demoralised. The waterway remained incomplete when Telford died on 2nd September, 1834 at the age of 77.

After yet more repairs to the earthworks the Birmingham and Liverpool finally opened to traffic on March 2nd, 1835 and a party of officials left Autherley Junction at 8 a.m. to traverse the canal. At a cost of £16,000 per mile it was one of Britain's most expensive waterways, but the main line of what was to become the Shropshire Union was at last finally complete.

An outstanding feature of the southern section of the "Shroppie" are its frequent and high embankments. These were called "valleys" by working boatmen. Here, on the outskirts of Market Drayton, an inter-war postcard view shows one of the many aqueducts needed by the canal to carry it along over the existing roadways that cross its route.

III : THE EVENTFUL YEARS : 1835-1914

While Telford was struggling to complete the Birmingham and Liverpool Junction through Shropshire, further to the north the merged Ellesmere and Chester companies were quietly getting on with the business of running their own canals. Theirs was an isolated and self-contained system of which the most northerly section – the Wirral line from Chester up to the River Mersey – was undergoing steady development. The terminal at Ellesmere Port provided the main focus for this activity.

By 1796 a passenger packet had been introduced between Chester and Liverpool. A succession of private operators paid rent to the company for the right to operate the franchise – this rising from £300 p.a. in 1800 to £1,300 p.a. by 1810, indicative of the steadily growing popularity of the route. Boats left Chester two hours before high water, so as to catch the tide at navigable state on the River Mersey. The return trip could well be guided back into the Ellesmere Port tidal basin by the lighthouse that still stands on the site today.

In the early days of the nineteenth century the terminal was a small and simple affair. At the foot of the lighthouse an unassuming building housed the passenger waiting room, cattle pens, and the piermaster's office. From the tidal basin the canal proper then began, climbing upwards by three locks. A wharf, small store, some stables and the lock-keeper's cottage comprised the buildings while a steam pumping engine lifted water to feed the wide dimensioned locks. These were large enough to accommodate 80 ton capacity Mersey flats – the barges that used the Wirral line and crossed to Liverpool. Some 60,000 gallons of water were used by a boat passing through. Although some water was supplied from the Chester canal this extra pumped water supply was soon found to be necessary as traffic built up.

Ellesmere Port was also seen as having a future beyond that of merely being a goods and passenger interchange between the canal and the Mersey. Attempts were made to turn it into a resort! Sea bathing was all the fashion at the turn of the century – and with the estuary a lot cleaner than it is today – bathing huts and archery butts were built. Such activities were promoted by both the canal carriers and inn keepers through into the 1820's. However it was evident that the real future lay with goods – particularly so when in 1826 the Act for the Birmingham and Liverpool Junction canal was passed. Telford, who having built the Wirral Line with Jessop, well knew the benefits that a main line from Birmingham to the Mersey would bring. He suggested various improvements for the terminus – and in 1828 got his orders. He was to undertake the building of a large warehouse and greatly extended transhipment facilities. With a route shorter by twenty miles and by thirty less locks than that provided by the alternative Trent and Mersey journey, the main line potential from Autherley Junction to Ellesmere Port was high.

This potential rapidly began to be realised. In the first six months of

The basin at Ellesmere Port, circa 1900. The transhipment docks were essential to the "Shroppie" and were used by a wide range of craft. "Paris" shows the livery used on the Shropshire Union Company boats – while in the background wide gauge barges as well as steam and sail powered coasters may also be seen.

1836 over 5,000 boats used the navigation. In the same year the Ellesmere and Chester Company took over the Mersey carrying operation from private traders — purchasing twenty-five Mersey flats. A steam tug was bought a year later. Ellesmere Port was growing rapidly, and at the expense of Chester — although this had been the river port the original company had sought to boost! By far the greatest part of the traffic was connected with the Staffordshire iron trade — ore and finished goods making up some 75% of the total tonnage carried in the early years. Despite the handicap of having to pay compensation tolls at its junction with the Trent and Mersey, the Middlewich branch was also beginning to do fair trade. Its strategic position in linking the rich dairy producing areas of Cheshire and Wales with the rapidly expanding city of Manchester was to serve it well.

The hoped for traffic from the Potteries also began to materialise and in 1844 a clay warehouse was added to the improvements being undertaken at Ellesmere Port. Steam haulage was introduced on the Wirral Line section — transhipment from narrow boats to the larger Mersey flats often being undertaken at Chester. The fall in packet boat traffic that took place in the early 1840's — largely as a consequence of railway competition — was being offset by the build up of the goods trade. In 1842 the Birmingham and Liverpool Junction company obtained powers to do more than just operate its own section of the route by getting Parliamentary approval to undertake carrying as well — while a year later the joint Ellesmere and

19

Chester Company celebrated the completion of its improvements to Ellesmere Port.

The re-development of the port had been completed under the direction of William Cubbit — for Telford had died some years earlier. As with the southern section of the main line he was thus deprived of seeing this completion of his last two major canal works. The centre piece of the undertaking was a great arched warehouse — built in the shape of a letter "E", straddling the water and allowing the handling of goods between an upper and lower basin. A large dock was integral to the development and it was planned that with due ceremony the various dignitaries would be carried on the steamer "Earl Powis" through the locks and into the new basin... but by a few inches the steamer proved too wide! Thus for the dignitaries — as it was to be with goods — "transhipment" had to take place. They re-embarked on the schooner "Bridget", the band played again — and the entrance was successfully made!

Keeping the canal open throughout the year often involved the use of the ice-breakers stationed at strategic points along the route. Here – circa 1900 – "Shroppie" employees from Audlem pose with their craft. The central hand rail was used to rock the boat from side to side when, hauled by a team of horses, it was crashed through the ice. The building – now the "Shroppie Fly" public house was originally a Company warehouse, the mounts of the now demolished 5 ton crane still visible on the wharf. Though a crane stands by the pub to-day it is of railway rather than canal origins – having been rescued from the nearby G.W.R. goods yard on the closure of Audlem station.

Despite these celebrations and jollifications the more informed and thinking members of the canal companies present must have been deeply worried. Their main line had been built too late. The long delayed opening of the Nantwich to Autherley Junction section meant that the canal had faced severe railway competition far earlier than had been expected.

Thirteen years earlier the Duke of Wellington, had opened the Liverpool to Manchester railway — "Rocket" showing the potential of this new transport system — while in 1837 the Grand Junction Railway had started operating between Liverpool and Birmingham. The canal owners were forced to adopt low carriage rates to compete and, although their traffic built up quite well, the effect on their revenue was dampening. In real terms the threat of railway competition had put the whole Birmingham to Liverpool scheme in jeopardy even before trading could begin properly.

Rumours spread. In 1833 there were constant stories of a large property owner in Cheshire offering £800,000 for the canal and that Stephenson's opinion had been consulted on the feasability of railway conversion. Although in the event it came to nothing this proposition must have seemed very attractive to those shareholders who had sunk considerable sums of money into a canal which was now foundering financially as well as physically slipping away at Shelmore. Sir John Wrottesley, an important Staffordshire landowner and a major shareholder, summed up the widespread view associated with railway conversion by remarking that "the idea of getting back all our money when I never expected a farthing is extremely tempting".

In the early 1840's, with the canal complete and Ellesmere Port extended, the time had come to take action. A merger between both companies on the main line could help cut costs and perhaps put matters on a sounder footing. In 1844 the discussions began and by August it was agreed that the "Ellesmere and Chester" would merge with the newer "Birmingham and Liverpool Junction". In May of 1845 the enabling Act passed through Parliament and the new Company was formed. However, this new concern was not to last for long — for even before permission for its establishment had been obtained discussions about railway conversion were once more taking place. By June the Company itself had set up its own Committee to investigate the possibilities.

1845 was the year of railway mania throughout the kingdom. Guided by the company engineer, W.A. Provis, the committee calculated that, by using the beds of canals as the basis for railway routes, conversion could be achieved at half the cost of building railways from scratch. The chance seemed too good to miss. Yet again the Company was re-constituted and in 1846 the Shropshire Union Railways and Canal Company came into being. The new name defined its plans. Three railways were to be built — one along the main line of the canal now barely ten years old. This Wolverhampton line from Calveley, near Chester, southwards to Norbury, would use Telford's cuttings and embankments. But the Ellesmere Port to Middlewich navigation was to be retained with an eye to the salt and pottery trades. Thus the original intention of the Chester Canal promoters had stood the test of time.

With parliamentary approval to build the one railway to Wolverhampton, another from Shrewsbury to Stafford and a third southwards from Crewe, the company was ready for a fresh start....but it was only to enjoy a few months of independence.... The rapidly expanding railways were set on achieving dominance of the transport field. The Grand Junction Railway that had threatened the canal main line from its very gestation, had itself been party to mergers. Now, as the London and North Western Railway with a route from London to the North Midlands, it saw the Shropshire Union, with its competing railway plans, as a very real threat. Accordingly in the autumn of 1846 it offered the canal company a perpetual lease. A rent equal to half the ordinary dividends of the L.N.W.R. was proposed. The canal directors were attracted by the "guarantee by a powerful Company of certain profits" and agreement was reached that management of the canals was to be in the hands of a joint committee. The Act was passed in 1847 and the L.N.W.R. assumed overall control of the Shropshire Union's affairs.

Between the years 1845-1847 the railway companies altogether took over nearly 1,000 miles of canal, sometimes closing them, sometimes converting them to routes — or as in the case of the Shropshire Union — using the canals as a buffer against competition and as a commercial feeder to their own systems.

Branches of the Shropshire Union led into Wales — while the main line of the canal ran through Chester. This was the edge of Great Western Railway country, and the L.N.W.R. was more than content to control waterways that deprived its rival of any potential income. By 1861 Robert Skey, then General Manager of the Shropshire Union, reckoned that the canal brought the L.N.W.R. as much as £60,000 trade annually. The railway company had also purchased the complex but busy Birmingham Canal Navigations — and this association helped generate traffic at the southern end of the canal. Of all the various Shropshire Union Railways and Canal Company conversion plans only one actually came to fruition. The Staffordshire to Shrewsbury railway line had been started before the L.N.W.R. lease had been agreed, so this was allowed to go ahead, the line being opened in 1849.

At last the Company's canals had some stability. After the tumultuous years of mergers, re-organisations and financial uncertainty the Shropshire Union found itself in a period of comparative calm. Paradoxically the railway had saved rather than destroyed these navigations. The L.N.W.R. treated the company well and — under the joint committee — it was allowed to operate virtually as a separate undertaking. In a period when canals generally were losing money, and in many cases going into liquidation, the "Shroppie" steadily built up its traffic. Trade directories of the time show

At the head of Northgate Locks in Chester, circa 1905. A Company-owned narrow boat prepares to descend the staircase locks, while in the background a broad-beamed barge pulls out into the cut. Wide boats such as these regularly worked from the Mersey down to Chester and as far south as Nantwich on the original broad section of the canal.

that in the 1850's goods could be "forwarded daily to all parts of the Kingdom", from the major wharves it served. Progress was steady. Well into the 1860's, and at a time when canals were out of favour and almost forgotten by the public, the Shropshire Union made good profits. Although these eventually fell away it still managed to earn enough to cover its operating costs — if not its debt interests — right through into the twentieth century.

It took until 1857 before all the legal niceties of establishing L.N.W.R. control were fully completed, but by 1849 the new dispensation was well underway. In that year the first leasing rentals were paid and the company established its own carrying fleet to operate over the whole of its system. From their own beginnings the railway companies had combined the twin functions of providing a route *and* undertaking carrying upon it. But not so with canals. Normal practice was that the canal company provided and maintained the route — income being derived from the tolls paid by the quite separate users. Various independent carriers had always operated on the waterways that became the Shropshire Union, but a tradition of undertaking their own carrying had been started by two of the constituent companies early on. In 1836 the Ellesmere and Chester company had taken over the Mersey traffic and had barges running down to Chester and beyond. In 1842 the more southerly Birmingham and Liverpool Junction Company had obtained powers to carry both passengers and goods — and unusually to offer haulage by steam tug to other users. The establishment of the Shropshire Union Railways and Canal Company as Carriers thus built on this background — and matched the dual "route and carriage" approach of its controlling railway company.

The fleet grew rapidly and offered a range of scheduled daily services. The faster fly boats provided a thirty-five hour passage between Birmingham and Ellesmere Port, and of twenty-four hours between Ellesmere Port and the Potteries. Similar runs were established elsewhere on the network. In 1870 the fleet comprised some 213 narrow boats and 65 "flats". It expanded rapidly throughout the seventies to reach 395 narrow boats, 101 "flats", 3 river and 5 canal tugs by 1889. By the end of the century over 70% of the trade on the Shropshire Union was being carried by its own boats — and this was to rise even higher in the following years.

From the start the canal had seen scheduled passenger runs but with the coming of the railways such traffic died away so that the Shropshire Union fleet was to become essentially a carrier of goods. Both the canal and its associated fleet had a strong Midland connection. Indeed the main line had been completed with the transport needs of Birmingham and the Black Country in mind. It was this area that provided the bulk of the early traffic and continued to do so for very many years. Iron ore and finished metal goods made up the greater part of this trade which, although fluctuating with the alternate booms and slumps of the industry, provided a continuing and central focus to carrying on the canal. Other cargoes built up to contribute to the increasing activities of the Shroppie. Clay and flint came in to Ellesmere Port for transhipment to the Potteries, finished china and pottery travelled back. Coal, so essential to nineteenth century England, was carried by the thousands of ton — as were all kinds of timbers and grain. Much of the traffic was comparatively local in origin. The mines of Shropshire and Staffordshire provided coal. Bricks and drainage pipes were manufactured on several sites along the Cheshire section to be transported and sold elsewhere. Cheese from the same county travelled across to Liverpool down to Birmingham and along the Middlewich branch towards Manchester, while limestone and slates from Wales came down the Llangollen branch to join the main line at Hurleston. In turn the modifications and extensions to terminals and transhipment points reflected the nature of this trade.

Above all Ellesmere Port was being developed. From the tiny transhipment point of the turn of the century it had, by 1830, become "a place of immense traffic". At this time about six hundred people lived and worked at what was rapidly becoming a company town. During the 1860's two new clay warehouses were built to cope with the expanding Potteries trade. In 1863 a gas-works was established at the port and this was eventually to supply the whole town. A large grain warehouse was opened in 1871 while the facilities for iron traffic handling were also extended. By 1875 severe overcrowding was being reported with boats having to wait several days before being unloaded — and in some cases having to take their trade elsewhere on the Mersey. Despite a high degree of mechanisation and the installation of hydraulic power handling systems the port was outgrowing the Telford extensions that had been conceived nearly half a century before.

The L.N.W.R. support continued, the railway company maintaining and improving the canal and its properties where needed. Much of the work had been under the direction of G.R. Jebb who — from a railway background — was appointed Chief Engineer to the Shropshire Union in 1869. At first his concerns were coping with the needs generated by this build up in traffic, despite which the canal was only just paying its way. However, the canal was to receive a new stimulus after 1885 with the authorisation of the Manchester Ship Canal. This re-kindled a general interest in canals but very specifically for the Shropshire Union and Ellesmere Port. The canal's outlet to the Mersey was to become part of the Ship Canal, the old direct route across to Liverpool thus being blocked. But large ships could now get down to the Port where previously the shifting Mersey mud banks had restricted traffic to smaller vessels. The L.N.W.R. invested heavily. Between 1870 and 1905 the railway company spent some £250,000 on the site. With its new quay, grain warehouse and dock and a high degree of mechanisation it became the most up to date canal terminus in the land. The town of Ellesmere Port was also transformed for new companies arrived to benefit from the combination of canal transport, railway and — via the ship canal — access to the sea. As if to emphasise the "Shroppie's" Midland connections these

The last large scale construction works on the "Shroppie" were extensions to Ellesmere Port. The Manchester Ship Canal was completed to the town in 1891 — a year later the extensions, here shown being built were carried out to allow the docking of sea going vessels. Telford's lighthouse at the entrance to the canal docks can be seen beyond the steam cranes and pile driver.

included the Wolverhampton Corrugated Iron Company, a major employer who came to the town in 1904. In the next five years three large flour mills were also established around the port — these importing grain from Canada and distributing milled products down the canal. Ellesmere Port had become a boom town.

In 1906 the Shropshire Union was able to report to the Royal Commission, which at that time was investigating waterways, that "large quantities of through traffic....pass over this navigation". Likewise a contemporary observer of 1910 noted "a going concern which is doing good service and is kept in a condition of high efficiency". The majority of trade was by the company's own boats — but about 20% of traffic was carried by bye-traders. The railway company, which had always kept the canal in good repair, was supporting its efficient operation to the full. In the early 1900's there was a daily service along the whole length of the main line. At Calveley south of Chester interchange sidings with the L.N.W.R. railway system had been established, and the junction at Barbridge was busy with goods leaving and joining via the Middlewich branch. The South Staffordshire trade also continued to generate traffic both to and from Autherley Junction.

Jebb's improvements throughout his period as Chief Engineer had ensured the canal's sound physical condition. He had increased the capacity of the Company's reservoirs, and had maintained tow paths, wharves and the canal itself all to high standards. It was reported that by 1914 "the canal.... was in a better condition of repair than it had ever been before".

But on August 4th, 1914 Britain declared war on Germany and the railway owned canals immediately came under the control of the Railway Executive Committee. The Indian summer of the Shropshire Union Railways and Canal Company was at an end.

IV : DECLINE : 1914-1968

The Shropshire Union entered the twentieth century as an effective and significant freight carrying concern, but the First World War soon dealt a severe blow to the network's viability and turned the modest pre-war surpluses into heavy losses. A combination of factors led to this deterioration. Although most boatmen remained on the water as essential workers the disruptive effects of war were soon to be felt. Wartime inflation, which forced up wage rates and other operating costs, quickly made carrying by the Company uneconomic. Changing attitudes towards working hours, conditions and pay also loomed ominously on the horizon threatening the canal industry as a whole. During the war the eight-hour day became more widespread and calls for a shorter working week were increasingly heard along the canals. For the boatmen who had enlisted in the armed forces, horizons were broadened and they discovered that there were more remunerative jobs available than on narrowboats. By the early 1920's the advent of road transport services also started to affect the canal's business. Some ex-boatmen took advantage of cheap ex-War Department vehicles to set up in business as road hauliers and so started taking traffic away from their former employer.

By the close of the Great War the L.N.W.R. had serious economic problems of its own so it did not relish resuming financial responsibility for the ailing Shropshire Union whose wartime losses had been borne by the Government. The application of the eight hour working day to the Company's boatmen made profitable carrying impossible. The controlling railway company insisted on drastic economy measures, and inevitably these included scrapping the Shropshire Union's carrying department. On June 1st., 1921 William Whittam, the then General Manager of the "Shroppie", issued the following closure notice from the Company offices at Tower Wharf in Chester.

"As the period of Government Control of the undertaking ceases on August 14th. next, the Company after serious consideration, much regrets to announce that it is found impossible to continue their carrying business under economic conditions".

The Company also gave notice that it would refuse to accept consignments for conveyance after August 31st. of that year — adding *"that until further notice the Waterway will be maintained in the hope that the Public will make use of it by their own or hired boats on payment of toll".*

Thus the Company's carrying services ended over the whole network including those across the Mersey from Ellesmere Port to Liverpool. As a further economy measure locks were closed on Sundays and were left unattended at night. The whole focus of the Company's operation was changed. The Shropshire Union's main source of income was now to come from the collecting of tolls. Ironically the wheel had come full circle — originally opened as a canal earning its sole income from such charges — the founding companies then embarked on their own carrying in the 1840's. The circumstances of the 1920's forced a return to a financial existence dependant on tolls.

A Cadbury's publicity picture taken at the stop lock at Knighton. The factory here opened in 1911, their fleet of narrow boats making regular collections for milk from the dairy farms of Shropshire.

The decision to cease carrying in 1921 had far reaching implications. In purely human terms over one thousand men were forced to seek new employment. A small number were taken on by the L.N.W.R. but many continued in the job they knew best — as boatmen. Richard Jones of Barbridge, who had joined the Shropshire Union in 1895 as a twelve-year old, found work with the Ceiriog Granite Company of Chirk and so was able to continue to ply the "Shroppie" delivering roadstone materials, — but many were less fortunate. The huge fleet of Company boats was disposed of, many being sold at rock bottom prices. It is said that so many boats awaited disposal at Nantwich Basin that it was possible to cross from one side of the water to the other by walking over their decks! The Ellesmere Port docks were leased to the Manchester Ship Canal and in 1922 the Shropshire Union was fully absorbed into the L.N.W.R. Even this was not to last for long for no sooner had this taken place than the railway grouping of 1923 brought the canal under the control of the London Midland and Scottish Railway.

The action taken by the Shropshire Union in 1921 eased its financial problems and a loss of £98,384 in 1921 was reduced to £26,473 in 1922 but although money was saved it was at the expense of the health of the canal. There was now a clear threat to the waterway's future because the Company's carrying department had been very aggressive and successful in winning traffic. Immediate deterioration was avoided because in many cases the cargoes formerly carried by the Company were taken over by existing and new bye-traders who continued to work on the route. Many Shropshire Union boats were purchased by individual boatmen who thus became their own "Number Ones". Others were sold to Companies such as A. & A. Peate Ltd., of Maesbury Hall Mill on the Llanymynech branch in Wales. This firm took over the carriage of grain from Ellesmere Port. New bye-traders such as the Chester and Liverpool Lighterage Company started carrying general merchandise and coal across the Mersey between these two cities. In 1922 a party of directors from the well known boat owning company of Fellows, Morton and Clayton carried out an exploratory voyage from Autherley Junction to Chester to survey the canal and its potential. They must have been satisfied for their boats began to make regular trips along the "Shroppie". Tonnage on the main line declined from 500,015 tons in 1923 to 433,230 tons by 1929. The remarkable thing is that the traffic remained so buoyant during a period that saw both the General Strike and considerable economic decline.

The year 1930 proved to be a watershed in the canal's history because from then onwards its role as a commercial-carrying route fell away. The lorry had demonstrated its potential during World War I and increasingly was seen to provide a cheap, fast convenient and flexible method of transporting goods. By the early 1930's motor transport was creating a mass exodus of traffic from both canals and railways. In the prevailing climate of economic depression cut-throat competition developed. The canals suffered the most because they were the least adaptable. On the "Shroppie" the challenge was met in the only possible way, by the Company cutting its tolls. But despite this action bye-traders found it almost impossible to remain competitive. Traffic fell away drastically in the bleak years of the 30's while in the 1940's many bye-traders abandoned the canal completely. Peates of Maesbury who had bought boats from the old "Shroppie" fleet were among those who abandoned the struggle, — going over to road transport in 1934. They gave as their reason the "greater convenience" of the lorry. Not all the lost canal traffic was won by road hauliers because the railways were equally keen to gain new custom. In the 1930's even the long established iron ore traffic from Ellesmere Port to the Midlands had started to be conveyed by rail.

With the outbreak of war in 1939 the canal once more came under Government control. Its decline briefly slowed down. The growth of the convoy system for merchant shipping re-vitalized the Mersey as an importing and transhipment centre — and the Shropshire Union provided a strategic line of communication from here to the Midlands. Although the main line was well used during the Second World War, its feeder canals west of Hurleston and Norbury Junctions saw very little commercial traffic. Even before the Second World War the controlling railway company, the L.M.S., seeing these canals as more of a liability than an asset, had considered their abandonment. The necessary Act was passed in 1944 — but a reprieve for the Llangollen section was eventually obtained as this provided an important source of drinking water for the reservoir at Hurleston.

The post-war years saw a bewildering series of changes in canal ownership and control — and a number of ill fated attempts to re-generate commercial traffic. When nationalisation came in 1947 the Shropshire Union became the responsibility of the Docks and Inland Waterways Executive of the British Transport Commission. But business continued to drift away. In 1948 Fellows, Morton and Clayton Ltd. went into voluntary liquidation because for every ton carried they were losing 1/- (5p.). A few years later the Thomas Clayton oil traffic also came to a halt. By the mid-1950's the British Waterways' North-West Divisional Fleet was the most sizeable carrier but in 1957 only 18,000 tons of goods arrived by canal at the Wolverhampton warehouses. The end was in sight for commercial carrying.

A variety of reasons contributed to the low level of use. Many complaints were made of high tolls imposed on canal users. In 1950 Messrs. Cowburn and Cowper Ltd. abandoned their bottleboats for the carriage of carbon disulphide from Manchester to Wolverhampton because the cost of the tolls alone were as much as the whole cost of delivery by road! Another weakness of canal transport was the need for transhipment which often involved the use of unsophisticated loading and unloading techniques. Road hauliers could provide a door to door service whereas canals needed to transfer goods to lorries for final delivery. Unfortunately from a commercial aspect the Shropshire Union passed through no major industrial towns which could generate profitable short-haul traffic. This meant that it was almost totally dependent on through cargoes from the Mersey to the Midlands. Good road and rail communication between these two areas made it

Following the disbanding of the Shropshire Union fleet in 1921 the well known firm of Fellows Morton and Clayton took over much of the carrying on the canal. Here at Ellesmere Port, circa 1930, a cluster of their narrow boats is tied up. The broad guage barges and flats also in the picture have almost certainly been unloading grain at the flour mill in the background.

increasingly difficult for the canal to begin to compete. The plight of the traders on the "Shroppie" was exacerbated by the growing shortage of north-bound cargoes which forced boats to engage in the wasteful practice of having to travel empty for half of any round-trip. Wage costs and crewing were other problem areas. The relative affluence of the 1950's led to increasing difficulties in finding good crews who were prepared to accept relatively low wages, long hours and the cramped cabins of canal boats as their homes. Rising wages could not be absorbed by increased productivity because of the fixed-tonnage capacity of the narrow boat.

By the 1950's the canal's decline was noticeable in its physical deterioration. Towpaths, which in the 1920's had been regularly topped with limestone chippings, became neglected and overgrown with the demise of horseboats. Wharves, warehouses and stables fell into disuse and disrepair. and even the once proud Ellesmere Port dock estate was closed by 1958. Commercial traffic along the "Shroppie" finally petered out in the late

1960's. After the British Waterways Board ceased carrying in 1963, Willow Wren Canal Transport Services and the Anderton Canal Carrying Company continued to take a few cargoes along the Shropshire Union. However, working narrow boats, became an infrequent sight between Ellesmere Port and Wolverhampton as traffic fell to a mere 4,000 tons by 1966. An interesting revival took place in the summer of 1968 when the Anderton Company began delivering silica sand from Weston Point Docks to Norbury Junction. Charlie Atkins, the boatman of Cadbury's fame worked this traffic for a time but it was short lived, mainly due to the cost of the unloading and subsequent road transport to a factory in Stafford. The last serious attempt to re-establish freight traffic on the canal took place in 1970 when the Birmingham and Midland Canal Carrying Company was awarded a contract for transporting oil from Ellesmere Port to Duckhams Depot at Aldridge near Walsall. This brave effort quickly ended in failure and it was obvious that the "Shroppie's" future now lay in the direction of recreation and its use by pleasurecraft. This had been formally recognised in 1968. The Shropshire Union was classified as a cruising waterway under the Transport Act of that year. A new era was underway.

Barbridge Junction 1957. These buildings, demolished the next year, at this stage carried the name Edward Dean and Sons, Millers of Chester. At one time, bearing the Shropshire Union Company name, they had been kept busy with the storage and transhipment of cheeses, malting barley, feed-stuffs and other agricultural commodities. The remains of the covered walkway that crossed the canal beneath the overall roof can just be seen. Rounding the turn is "Kidsgrove" one of the twelve "station boats" produced by British Waterways in the mid 1950s – cabin conversions of ex Birmingham area day boats.

V : BOATS AND CARGOES

Watching the holiday and hire craft on the "Shroppie" today, it is easy to forget that this long length of water was once part of a transport revolution. Far from being built for leisure it was constructed by hard headed merchants who saw the waterway as an economic and efficient means of moving goods.

As with most other canals the early days of the Shropshire Union saw passenger as well as goods traffic — but by the time the young company had founded its own carrying fleet in 1845 passenger traffic was dying away. The rapid transit offered by railways was proving far superior to the speed of even the fastest "fly boats". But despite the ever increasing mileage of the railways and their slow erosion of canal goods traffic well laden narrow boats plied the length of the "Shroppie" for over a century. These collected and delivered goods along the rural sections, made connections with the London North Western Railway at rail-canal interchanges, and served the needs of factories deep in the Black Country. Even as late as the 1960's, it was possible to occasionally glimpse the Shropshire Union fulfilling its original purpose by providing a waterway for commercial traffic.

When Telford planned the Birmingham and Liverpool Junction to complete the main line route from Ellesmere Port to Wolverhampton above all else he saw the canal as providing for long distance traffic. From the very start iron goods became the waterway's staple trade. By 1870 over a third of the company's fleet of 213 boats was employed in the carriage of iron ore and finished metal goods. Castings and girders from the Staffordshire iron towns went north. Iron ore provided loads for the boats coming south. Later in the century the clatter of corrugated iron became a familiar sound at both ends of the Shroppie. The Wolverhampton Corrugated Iron Company — itself later to move up the canal and re-locate at Ellesmere Port — sent thousands of tons of roofing and building sheets to the Mersey for export. Loads that had descended Audlem Locks and crossed the Cheshire Plain a few months earlier were to become the roofs and walls of shanty towns in the outback and gold rush settlements of North America, Australia and other colonies.

The Shropshire iron making district around Coalbrookdale also took advantage of the canal to distribute its products. The Lilleshall Company, owned by the Duke of Sutherland, had its own warehouses at Norbury Junction. Here goods brought in by tub-boats along the Newport Branch, were transferred to narrow boats to travel north.

The importance of iron traffic on the canal was reflected in the provision of excellent facilities at Ellesmere Port, — a new warehouse being built there in 1884 to store such products before transhipment and passage abroad. Unfortunately the canal was heavily dependent upon a type of traffic which suffered from cyclical booms and slumps. In many reports

TO TRADERS.

BIRMINGHAM AND LIVERPOOL JUNCTION CANAL NAVIGATION.

NOTICE is hereby given, that on Monday the second day of March next, the Trade will be permitted to pass *along the whole line of the Canal* from the Staffordshire and Worcestershire Canal at Autherley, to the Ellesmere and Chester Canal at Nantwich, passing through Brewood, Wheaton Aston, Lapley, Church Eaton, Gnosall, Market Drayton, and Audlem; and also *along the Newport Branch Canal*, passing from the main line of Canal at Norbury, through the town of Newport, to the Shrewsbury Canal near Wellington.

Wharfage ground will be found at Chillington, Dean's Hall, Brewood, Watling Street Road, near Ivetsey Bank, Wheaton Aston, Church Eaton, Gnosall, Norbury Junction, Adbaston, Cheswardine, Market Drayton, Adderley, Audlem, and Nantwich; also at Newport, and at the Shrewsbury Canal Junction.

By order of the Committee,

THOS. EYRE LEE, Clerk,

W. CUBITT, Principal Engineer.

69, Newhall-street, Birmingham, }
February 2, 1835. }

N.B. Rates of Tonnage are on all Coal, Iron, and other articles (except Lime) one penny per ton per mile, and on Lime one halfpenny per ton per mile; and any Traders requiring information may apply to Mr. R. S. SKEY, jun. Collector of Tolls, Canal Office, Newport, Salop.

Published in 1835 this notice to traders shows the importance of coal and iron carriage in the early economy of the "Shroppie". The wording suggests a mixture of fatigue and relief in that – at last – traffic was able to pass "along the whole of the Canal" after all the difficulties and delays involved in completing this final southern section of the main line.

to shareholders the Company attributed declining profits to "the iron trade falling off". But usually it picked up again! Nevertheless the iron trade was of double benefit for it provided a natural back carriage in the form of iron ore. The mid nineteenth century saw the adoption of the Bessemer steel making process in the Black Country — and this required an iron ore low in phosphorous. Such ores came in from Sweden and also by coaster from Cumberland. A special wharf was built at Ellesmere Port for transhipment from the sea going vessels to narrow boats before the ore could continue southward on its journey to the steelworks of Staffordshire. Canal traffic fell away generally in the twentieth century and iron was no exception. However, until the very close of commercial carrying it formed a significant proportion of "Shroppie" traffic — and as late as the mid 1940's metals of various types were the dominant materials carried over the route.

Coal was also a valuable cargo for the Shropshire Union. Indeed the first ever traffic on the Chester Canal was a coal boat to Beeston in 1775, whilst the opening of the Wirral Branch in 1795 allowed Mersey flats to bring Lancashire coal to the Tower Wharf at Chester. When the Birmingham and Liverpool opened in 1835, coal traffic immediately became prominent. Eddowe's Salopian Journal noted on 11th. March of that year that "one of the first boats to use the Birmingham and Liverpool was one carrying coal from the Shropshire Collieries to Market Drayton".

While much of this coal was for domestic use, deliveries were also made to canalside industries. These included the steam-powered mills of Chester and elsewhere — while the Cadbury's factory at Knighton was also regularly supplied by the canal with Staffordshire dug coal until well into the late 1930's.

Many Shropshire Union boats were engaged in shipping limestone. This originated in Welsh quarries such as those at Trevor and Llanymynech and came down onto the main line at Hurleston Junction. A typical "stone" boat was the "Iron Duke" which in 1879 was regularly running from Pontcysyllte to Wolverhampton where the limestone was used as a flux in the iron industry. Like other boats in this trade it also conveyed lime which was a vital commodity to Victorian farmers before the widespread adoption of modern fertilizers. Many a cargo of lime was delivered by boat to be spread on the rich grasslands of Shropshire and Cheshire — for as well as linking an industrial area with the sea the "Shroppie" also served an extensive agricultural community.

The agricultural traffic was considerable — and boats laden with grain and cattle feed were an everyday sight on the "Shroppie" until after the First World War when the increased use of lorries began to undermine this trade. In the early days grain would be transported to local mills and feedstuffs on to the local farms. With the coming of the large steam mills in the second half of the nineteenth century imported grain also started to be carried — but the real change came with the opening of the Manchester Ship Canal followed by the establishment of the large mills at Ellesmere

Port in the early twentieth century. In 1899 the Manchester Ship Canal Company had opened a six storey grain warehouse and by the First World War 70% of its through put was being carried inland by the canal. Combined with the existing output of the mills this traffic formed a significant proportion of "Shroppie" carrying in the early days of the twentieth century. Even after the Second World War grain and flour continued to make up a high proportion of Shropshire Union tonnage. Many of the bye-traders on the canal were either millers or were connected with the corn trade — and some took over the long distance hauling of such commodities when the company fleet was disbanded. Among them were such traders as William Owen of Barbridge who operated two boats on the Ellesmere Port to Birmingham run throughout the 1920's. His loads were mainly of wheat and flour.

The farmlands of Shropshire and Cheshire produced both grain and milk and two important cargoes derived from these were malt and cheese. Ellesmere boasted a notable malting industry in the nineteenth century and rapid fly boats carried the malt over the Middlewich Branch to the Lancashire breweries. These fast boats were also on hand at places like Whitchurch, Nantwich and Market Drayton during the cheese fairs and good care had to be taken of this perishable commodity. White cloths covered the boats to keep the heat off the cheese — and at Nantwich Basin special warehousing facilities were available.

The cheese traffic continued well into this century. Every Saturday morning up to about 1920 a cheeseboat was loaded at Audlem. It was a common sight to see the road down to the wharf full of farm carts bringing the week's making of cheese to be sent off to Manchester.

Heavy, bulky and awkward commodities like timber were well suited to water transport. In 1879 the general merchant, Henry Belcher, began to employ one of his boats, in the carriage of imported softwoods from Ellesmere Port to his depot at Gnosall in Staffordshire. The canal also carried English hardwoods like oak from their place of felling to the sawmills. Much of this traffic originated in Wales. The Llangollen branch was completed in 1805 and Eddowe's Salopian Journal of 7th January 1806 noted that "six vessels heavy laden with oak timber from the Ellesmere Canal, having passed along the old Chester Canal, arrived at the Tower Wharf in Chester on Monday last, the first that have gone by the conveyance since the communication between these canals was opened".

The original plan of the Chester Canal promoters was that they should capture some of the Staffordshire pottery trade from the Trent and Mersey Company via the route to Middlewich. Although this plan was delayed by very many years the Shropshire Union eventually managed to provide a very valuable service to the Potteries — and by the 1850's the determined efforts of the Shropshire Union company to obtain a proportion of this trade were beginning to pay off. Cornish china clay was transhipped into narrow boats at Ellesmere Port and — via the then

A postcard view – circa 1910 – of the wharf at Market Drayton. Coal predominates in this picture but the cranes, small office and surprisingly modern looking warehouse handled a wide range of agricultural and domestic commodities for the district.

new branch to Middlewich — taken on to Stoke-on-Trent. The boats returned laden with crated crockery bound for export — the water providing a relatively safe shock free transport for this fragile commodity. Clay warehousing was built at Ellesmere Port — and in 1905 over 24,000 tons of potters materials were handled by the Company.

Apart from these staple cargoes all manner of goods passed over the "Shroppie" ranging from sugar to lead, from beer to wooden chairs. 80,000 tons of general merchandise were being handled annually at the start of the twentieth century and fast fly boats maintained regular daily services to carry these miscellaneous cargoes. Among these a regular load of Guinness passed down the "Shroppie" for many years — en route from Dublin to the Midlands.

Vigorous house building in the Victorian period was reflected in numerous consignments of bricks, pipes and slates many of which were destined for Lancashire. In 1879 Edward Griffiths carried slates from Chirk to Barbridge in his boat "Lydia", whilst "Perseverance" was engaged in shipping bricks and pipes from Rowley Regis in the West Midlands to Manchester.

A central aspect of cargo carrying was the provision of wharves and warehouses where the goods could be handled and stored. The company had its own depots at many places including Chester, Nantwich and Market Drayton — supervised by their own agents. Private carriers could use these facilities on payment of wharfage, craneage and warehouse charges. Where boats to be unloaded were carrying perishable cargoes these would use the under cover facilities. The surviving canal warehouse at Market Drayton is an excellent example of such a building. Although cranes were sometimes used for unloading, a good deal of manual work was required of the crew, shovels and wheelbarrows usually being used. Warehousemen then supervised the storing of goods and their distribution within the locality.

The Company employed agents at all major points on the canal. The Post Office Directory of Shropshire for 1856 lists William Tomkinson as the Shropshire Union's agent at Market Drayton. His appointment was only part-time because he was also a dealer in corn, slate and guano which no doubt he brought in by canal. His colleagues along the cut included Benjamin Clay, who served the company for over a quarter of a century at Nantwich, and a resident agent, Fred Greensell, at the important junction at Barbridge.

Wharves were located at frequent points along the canal to serve the local communities and the one at Goldstone near Cheswardine was as typical as any. A small unpretentious looking warehouse was built here and in the 1850's the local beer seller James Wild, acted as wharfinger. As well as the local traffic in agricultural goods, "Joey" boats from the Black Country unloaded coal at Goldstone which was then carted away to the surrounding houses and farms.

When the London and North Western Railway Company obtained its lease of the Shropshire Union it did so on the basis of a shrewd appraisal of its own situation. It provided a railway trunk route from London through the Midlands to the North West — but saw that it could well do with feeder lines from the commercial and industrial heartlands of Birmingham and South Staffordshire as well as protection to the west where the rival Great Western Railway came up on its Welsh flank. Existing canals could provide some answers. In 1846 the Birmingham Canal Navigations also came under the control of the L.N.W.R. This was an extensive system with numerous branches into Staffordshire, Warwickshire and Worcestershire. To list but a few of the places it served sounds like an industrial Midlands roll call. Birmingham itself, Smethwick, Oldbury, Dudley, Tipton, Bilston and Wolverhampton all were on the B.C.N. waterway system and were likely to generate traffic for the railway. A year later the lease of the Shropshire Union Company was agreed. The western side, with branches into the mineral rich areas of north east Wales, was in part secured against the G.W.R., while access to the Mersey was also achieved.

For the next sixty years and more the railway company looked upon these canals as natural extensions to their own system. With hindsight it is easy to suggest that their potential was never fully developed by the L.N.W.R. — but faith *was* kept with the waterways and the "Shroppie", along with the B.C.N. to its south, was to benefit from steady, if cautious investment and from careful maintenance. Under the watchful eye of

George Jebb, who served the two canal systems as Chief Engineer for fifty years, the physical state of the "Shroppie" was steadily improved. In Bradshaw's "Canal and Navigable Rivers" of 1904 de Salis observed that although "the draught of water.... is less than that prevailing generally on narrow boat canals....the works are well maintained".

As well as caring for the canal itself, attention was also given to the Company fleet and its horses. Many "Shroppie" narrow boats were built either at its own yard in Chester or along the Llangollen branch at Welsh Frankton and Pontcysyllte. Others were also built at independent yards in the south Midlands, while some steel hulled boats were even built by the L.N.W.R. at its railway workshops in Crewe.

The fleet was made up of a variety of craft. The broad gauged northern end of the canal saw traffic being carried by Mersey flats. These large wide boats worked from Ellesmere Port to Chester as well as on the river itself, and occasionally would travel as far south as Nantwich. "Ruby" was such a vessel — built in the 1870's at Chester, 72 feet long with bluff bows, flat bottom and rounded bilges, she could carry a cargo of 54 tons. On her foredeck she was fitted with a large windlass to handle the anchor cables needed on the tideway of the Mersey — together with a smaller one to work the long warps used as the boat was manoeuvred around the docks. By 1900, the company had about a hundred such flats — together with a handful of tugs used to work them on the canal and on the Mersey. However, when the fleet was disbanded in 1921, along with the other boats, "Ruby" was put up for sale. Acquired by the local firm of Abels she was used as a grain carrier. She was re-named "Mossdale", and underwent a major re-build in the 1930's and fortunately is now preserved back in her original home — at The Boat Museum, Ellesmere Port.

By the early twentieth century the Shropshire Union had a total fleet of well over four hundred boats, the majority of these being traditional horse drawn narrow boats. Typical of such a vessel was "Rambler", Boat Number 174, registered at Nantwich on 9th. January 1879. Thomas Davis was her master and her owners are shown as being the Shropshire Union Railways and Canal Company of Chester. Although the overall head office was officially located at Euston Station on the premises of the controlling L.N.W.R. the head office of the canal as such remained in Cheshire. "Rambler" is recorded as having mainly been used for stone traffic, so no doubt the majority of her voyages included travelling the branch from Hurleston into Wales and the quarries at Trevor. Interestingly the register records her as being a "Horse drawn narrow boat — **not** to be used as a fly boat".

The "Shroppie", from its earliest days, ran fast scheduled trips by fly boat. The express traffic of the canal — these craft ran to a strict timetable and to help them maintain this they were given rights of way over all other boats. Black roundels painted on their white bow panels helped identify them as they were rushed along — often at a canter — by

The turn of the century and the crowed dock of Ellesmere Port. The iron ore wharf to the left, flour mill to the centre and clay warehouse to the right generated traffic for the wide range of boats seen here. They include a topsail schooner, steam coaster, Mersey flats and Company narrow boats.

teams of selected horses. Every Tuesday and Saturday afternoon, promptly at 5.00 p.m., a "Shroppie Fly" would leave Birmingham en route for Ellesmere Port, there to complete the journey just twenty-nine hours later. A brief turn-around of four hours was allowed, so that by 2.00 a.m. in the dark of the following morning the boat would be hurrying southwards again. Fresh horses were provided at approximately twenty mile intervals — change over points being arranged at Autherley Junction, Norbury Junction, Tyrley and Bunbury, as well as at the two termini. The boats themselves were built with speed in mind and were designed for cargoes of up to 18 tons, rather than the more normal loads of 25 tons. The upper planks of the hulls curved in, while the steep rake of their sterns emphasised an overall concern for speed. Fly boats were used for perishable goods and general merchandise, rather than the bulkier cargoes of stone, coal and grain as carried by the slower ordinary traffic on the canal.

L.T.C. Rolt's famous "Narrow Boat" was an ex Shroppie fly. Like so many others with her the "Cressy" was sold out of the Company when it ceased carrying — in her case to be bought by a firm of millers on the Welsh branch of the system. After several years of carrying coal she was eventually bought and converted for cruising. Finally broken up in the early 1950's, her remains were burned. However, a fine model of the Shroppie fly "Haig" is displayed at The Boat Museum and provides a good visual reminder of the appearance of these famous working boats.

Except for some steam tugs working on the northern sections of the canal the Shropshire Union Company relied on horses for motive power throughout its carrying life. Steamers had been introduced on some other canals by the late 1880's — while the Shroppie carried out its own unusual experiment with locomotive hauling around this time. In the early twentieth century semi-diesel engines began to be generally used — but although the "Shroppie" briefly experimented with an internal combustion engine in a boat called "Waterlily" the horse remained supreme. Well funded, by comparison with some of the bye-traders and smaller carrying firms, the Shropshire Union was able to buy good horses and to care for them well. Over three hundred animals were in work by 1900 — the majority being used to haul narrow boats, but a significant number pulled the drays and vans that carried goods to and from the wharves. The horse requires regular feeds and adequate stabling. Along the main line a string of company stables catered for such needs. A well restored stable block can be seen at Ellesmere Port while others in good external condition can be found at Bunbury, Hack Green and on the Middlewich branch near Church Minshull. At Audlem the stable that still stands at the foot of the lock flight was used to house the extra horses found necessary to work the boats through the climb. Horses usually worked some twenty five miles a day on a diet of hay, peas, oats and chaff — the water they needed being taken from the canal. Tow paths were kept in sound condition on the "Shroppie", white limestone chippings carried down from Wales forming a distinctive walk way. Towards the end of horse hauling days the firm of Thomas Clayton of Olbury shod its horses with special shoes to enable them to get a good grip on this nobbled but well draining surface.

When the Shropshire Union abandoned carrying the well known firm of Fellows Morton and Clayton took over much of the carriage of goods along the line, while various bye-traders bought ex Company boats to add to the traffic that still plied the canal.

Prominent amongst other canal users was Cadbury's, the famous chocolate making company. In the early years of this century they launched a new brand called "Dairy Milk" and as part of their vigorous expansion programme a milk evaporating plant was established in 1911 at Knighton just a few miles north of Norbury Junction. Cadbury's used their own smart wooden horse-drawn boats to collect milk from canalside loading points between Autherley and Adderley, thus tapping the rich dairying countryside around. At Knighton this local supply of milk was evaporated and then was added to cocoa-bean powder and sugar to produce "chocolate crumb". This formed a partly processed chocolate which kept well and could be transported to Bournville, via the Birmingham and Worcester Canal, there to be made into finished chocolate.

Two special motor boats were constructed to serve the new factory "Bournville I" being launched in 1911, "Bournville II" joining her a year later. These were unusual vessels in a number of ways and were the first motor boats ever to be operated on English canals. Of normal narrow boat dimensions — as indeed they had to be to work the route to Bournville — they were built of mild steel plate rather than the more usual oak and elm. Each boat had two rudders, one on either side of the propellor, in an attempt to minimise wash and bank erosion. Steering was by wheel rather than tiller and power was obtained from 15 hp Bolinder semi-diesel oil engines manufactured in Sweden. Rather than the usual "cloths" the cargoes were covered by water tight steel decks running the whole length of the boats. Loading and unloading was by hatchway. These boats made a round trip of about a week. A fifteen hour journey took them to Bournville where they unloaded their cargoes of crumb. They next crossed to Worcester to join the River Severn and travelled down to the docks at Gloucester. Loaded up with sugar they would then turn north once more, entering the Staffordshire and Worcester Canal at Stourport. At Autherley Junction the "Shroppie" would be re-joined and the return to Knighton made. The motors proved very successful and Bolinder engines were adopted by many other users — but the structural design of the two "Bournvilles" was not up to the heavy conditions met. The brave experiment ended when they were eventually replaced by conventional wooden motor boats. When Cadbury's disbanded its own carrying fleet in 1928 the wooden "milk boats" — which each carried 150 churns up and down on their milk runs — were replaced by lorries — while Fellows Morton and Clayton took over the carriage of chocolate "crumb". Other journeys were made to Ellesmere Port with finished chocolate products with sugar and cocoa beans being returned as backcarriage. After nationalisation British Waterway took over the Knighton service, and it was not until 1961 that the last cargo of chocolate "crumb" traversed the "Shroppie" on a final waterways journey to Bournville

Another well known fleet of boats which regularly worked the length of the main line was that of Thomas Clayton's of Oldbury. This Birmingham based firm specialised in the transport of liquid cargoes and from the 1920's until the mid 1950's their craft plied the "Shroppie", mainly being used in the carriage of fuel oil from the Stanlow refinery near Ellesmere Port to Shell's depot at Langley Green near Birmingham. This traffic began in 1924 and the horse boats normally completed the round trip of one hundred and sixty miles within the week. In 1938 Clayton's began introducing motors on this route but some horse-drawn boats survived until as late as 1953. From a post-war peak of 30,000 tons in 1946, oil traffic

The Cadbury's factory at Knighton provided much "Shroppie" traffic; milk, sugar, cocoa, chocolate crumb and coal being shipped along the canal. Boats in the small Company fleet were all named "Bournville" but numbered separately. Very well maintained, they were finished in a distinctive and attractive maroon livery.

steadily declined until in 1954 only 12,000 tons were carried. Eight pairs of boats were then in use but in the following year Shell declined to renew their contract and the autumn of 1955 saw Clayton's attractively decorated boats make their own final journeys along the canal.

Clayton motor boats were named after rivers and the "Severn" was a regular on the Shroppie run. Likewise, the motor "Dove" could often be seen laden with about 20 tons of fuel oil while hauling a butty boat such as "Gifford" with her own cargo of 25 tons aboard. "Gifford" survives. She has been beautifully restored and is owned by The Boat Museum. There she now lies, in the Ellesmere Port basin she so often passed during her working life.

Along with the Cadbury's and Clayton boats the Fellows Morton and Clayton craft were prominent on the Shroppie after the Company relinquished its own carrying operations. Until the 1920's the "Joshers" as the F.M.C. boats were affectionately known, did not regularly operate on the Shropshire Union but used the neighbouring Trent and Mersey for runs to Manchester and the north. The Fellows Morton and Clayton boats employed on the "Shroppie" were based at the Albion Wharf in Wolverhampton but many worked through to Birmingham and unloaded at the Crescent Wharf. Cargoes were varied and considerable from the 1920's until 1948 when the Company ceased trading. They included sugar, metals such as copper and aluminium, hardwoods, paraffin wax for candlemaking, resin in kegs, tripoli powder and flour.

After the demise of Fellows Morton and Clayton the British Waterways monopolised most of the traffic in the 1950's but their operations became increasingly uneconomic. The traditional cargoes of the Shroppie continued to pass along the canal until commercial carrying finally petered out during the 1960's.

A pair of Clayton tanker boats negotiate Northgate Locks, Chester. Familiar craft on the "Shroppie" these colourful boats made regular runs from the Shell Oil refinery at Stanlow down to Langley Green, Birmingham for the thirty years between 1925 and 1955.

VI : LIFE ON THE "SHROPPIE"

As commercial carrying died away on the "Shroppie", so also did a traditional way of life. From the beginnings of the canal age the boat people had developed their own nomadic life style. Living apart from the great mass of the population and ever on the move, the cramped cabins of their narrow boats serving as home for whole families, theirs of necessity was a distinctive and separate existence. This relatively isolated life bred its own attitudes and traditions and a closely knit largely self-contained community was formed of those whose work meant their lives were spent almost permanently on the waterways.

Richard Jones of Barbridge started work on the "Shroppie" in 1895. He was then aged twelve and worked for the carrying department of the Company until its closure in 1921. His life on the cut continued however, for he next obtained employment with a firm on the Llangollen branch and worked on boats carrying limestone on Shropshire Union waters until the Second World War. Len Wilson of Walsall was born in 1901. His father was a Shropshire Union employee before him and Len followed him into the Company in 1914. He also was forced to leave its direct employment in the upheaval of 1921 — but was taken on by the carrying firm of Thomas's of Walsall. He thus continued to do many trips along the length of the "Shroppie" — often up from the Midlands, then round to Welshpool via Hurleston Junction. His carrying days on the canal continued until the late 1940's. It is the personal reminiscences of such boatmen as these that provide us with a glimpse of what working life on the "Shroppie" was really like in the first part of the twentieth century.

It was a hard life and the hours were long. The "Shroppie", with its regular services of fast "fly boats", made particular demands. Crews of four worked these boats in shifts — and with very tight schedules there was hardly a stop except to change horses. On the family run boats life was less hectic but no easier. Well into the 1940's Clayton horse boats would be on the move from 4 a.m. in the thin light of dawn — right through until 10 p.m. at night.

Bad weather rarely stopped the boats. On bleak winter days crews would become wet and cold, whilst on Telford's exposed embankments such as Shelmore and Shebdon it was almost impossible to make progress during a north easterly gale when the canal's usually placid water was whipped up into waves. Only a spell of severe freezing brought traffic to a complete halt. Len Wilson recalls being trapped in thick ice at Audlem town lock for over a month in 1917. "Me and a youth could walk across the canal and the ice was 10½ inches thick. I measured it for myself". The long hard winter of 1962-63 also brought traffic on the "Shroppie" to a total halt and sounded the death knell for commercial carrying on the canals. The Shropshire Union in common with most other companies, boasted several ice boats strategically stationed along the route. With a team of horses pulling and a dozen men rocking the icebreaker from side to side, it was a splendid sight and sound as these boats smashed a channel through the ice.

The regulars on the "Shroppie" knew its every twist and turn and found little difficulty in navigating at night without lights. Such were their boat handling skills that accidents were rare. In forty years of work on the canal Richard Jones can only remember one fatality – this when a boatman drowned in a lock at Audlem. As Company reports show, accidents were often associated with horses. Len Wilson recalls how Tommy Littlehales was leading his horse past the warehouse at Wheaton Aston. The animal shied at something in the water and pinned the unfortunate boatman against the spindle of the ½ ton crane on the wharf. Tommy Littlehales suffered rib injuries from which he subsequently died.

Some of the "Shroppie" ghost stories reflect such accidents. The high bridge in Grub Street cutting is said to have its own resident spectre. Ever since a man was drowned in the cut, early in the century, a black monkey-like figure with white eyes has been reported as have been frequently seen in the area. Likewise Tyrley middle lock is reported to be haunted. If you come up to it in the middle of the night the local ghost will push the lock gates shut behind your boat!

Until its demise in 1921, the Shropshire Union Carrying Department paid its captains on the basis of the tonnage carried per mile. This piecework system encouraged the boatmen to do as much work as possible – and holidays were rarely taken because they were unpaid. The captain had to employ his own mate to help him run the boat and, although some "Shroppie" masters took their families along with them, this was by no means popular. For example Richard Jones's wife normally lived in their Company cottage at Barbridge and she would only take to the boat if the mate was too ill to work.

A life centred on the self contained world of the "cut" made for much inter-marriage among the boaters – and many "Shroppie" workers had associations with the canal extending back over decades. Second and third generations of Shropshire Union employees were common and most members of a crew could expect to meet a brother-in-law or a cousin or an uncle somewhere along the length of the main line. As boats passed one another on the cut voices would be raised to exchange family news and gossip as long as the moving boats remained in earshot. Such close ties made for a shy and reserved attitude towards strangers – but for warm and friendly relationships within the boating community. Nicknames were common within this private world. There was "Vinegar Joe", "Peggy Albert" with his wooden leg, "80 Ton" Tom Wilby (did he overload his boat?) and Joe "Soap" who rarely managed to wash! When Mary Ann spoke it was noted that one side of her mouth went up far more than the other. Thus "Mary Ann Stretch-It" got her name! "Jack the Snipe" was an accomplished boxer – while "Harry the Tar" was the well known master of a Clayton tanker boat on the run from Shrewsbury gas works via Norbury Junction to Oldbury. Among the better

A boatman, in traditional corduroy trousers, waistcoat and cap, leads his horse drawn boat through a "rocking" – the term used for the steep sided cuttings on the southern section of the canal. Horses often worked throughout the day, eating from nose tins suspended from their harness as they went.

known of the more recent "Shroppie" boatmen was Charlie Atkins – who carrying chocolate crumb from Knighton for some 13 years became widely known as "Chocolate Charlie".

Leisure time was limited. In the evenings the boaters would find their relaxation at such canal side inns as the Trooper at Christleton, the Jolly Tar at Barbridge and the Bridge Inn at Audlem. In the early 1900's with beer at only 3 pence a pint the pubs however served as more than mere ale houses. Within their walls developed a unique folk culture which sufficed to lighten the rigours of the boater's lives. Before the First World War inns like the Anchor at High Offley had a score of narrow boats tied up outside in the evenings, with horses filling the stables. Over forty men and women would pack the tiny taproom telling stories, step-dancing or singing their favourite songs whilst the concertina played in the background. Mrs. Lily Pascall, who was licensee of the "Anchor" until the 1960's knew her clients well. Her own husband, George, worked on the Cadbury's milk boats during the 1920's and "Shroppie" characters such as Reuben Thomas, Moses Hamer and Samuel Boaz all formed important members of the "Shroppie" canal community who shared life on the waterway. On long still summer days this life was undoubtedly pleasant but the craggy weatherbeaten faces of the surviving boatmen shows that it could also be demanding and harsh. A shared life made for peaceable and friendly relationships generally — but the occasional fight or family fued was not entirely unknown. However Lily Pascall who served the crews with their beer for over sixty years remembers them as a "lovely people". Richard Jones bears this out, for after many years on the "Shroppie" he described his fellow boaters as "a good class of people who would always help one another when in trouble".

Apart from their own traditional way of life the boat crews were also identifiable by their dress. Woollen cord trousers and a jacket was the usual outfit for men — who invariably wore a peaked cap or trilby. In summer a moleskin waistcoat and a white shirt with sleeves rolled up provided a more comfortable attire. Even until the 1930's the women usually wore dark ankle length skirts with a plain or striped blouse. A distinctive long white apron was also customary while bonnets or shawls afforded protection in all weathers. For years a shop at Ellesmere Port docks did good trade selling these traditional clothes as well as boating stores and equipment.

The traditions of this way of life extended to the boats themselves. The relatively subdued livery of the Shropshire Union boats included black side panels to the cabins, marked with the name of the company, while distinctive white gunwales bore the names of the individual craft engraved on their sterns. Doors to cabins normally carried the familiar roses and castles. Following 1921 Fellows Morton and Clayton boats became the most common craft. Dark cabin side panels also featured on their vessels — but boat names were carried in white on dark gunwales. Most colourful of all the regular "Shroppie" boats were the tankers belonging to Thomas Clayton of Olbury. On these red cabin panels predominated, the company and boat names being picked out in white. Lozenges and other patterns in red, yellow and blue emphasised the overall impression of cheerfulness as if to compensate for the drab tars and heavy oils carried within.

Serving the dual purpose of carrying vehicle and floating home the boats presented a challenge to the women who had to housekeep and raise a family in the cramped accommodation of a tiny cabin. And tiny indeed they were. A typical family boat belonging to the Shropshire Union Company fleet, the "Napier", provides an example. "Napier" was measured and inspected at Nantwich on 22nd. March 1889. The cabin was found to be 4'10" high, 8'6" long and 5'10" wide. This minute space was formally

The lockkeeper at Audlem, dressed in his railway company uniform, emerges from his cottage. "Shroppie" employees included boatmen, office staff, warehousemen, boatbuilders, maintenance gangs, stablemen, even molecatchers as well as a small Company police force.

registered as providing suitable living accommodation for two adults and two children!

Canal Boat Acts had been passed in 1877 and 1884 demanding that boats were measured, inspected and registered so as to ensure that certain minimum standards of space and hygiene were maintained. The number of permitted dwellers was fixed in accordance to the free air space within the cabin. 60 cubic feet of air was allowed per adult, 40 cubic feet for a child. With but a few boats providing room for more than three or four people, many a canal child must have been hidden in the bushes along the Shroppie tow paths when an Inspector was sighted drawing near! Some boats — such as "Gifford", the Clayton tar boat now preserved at Ellesmere Port — boasted an extra cabin in the bows — but as these took up precious cargo space extra cabins were comparatively rare. The Inspectors appointed to enforce the Canal Boat Acts both measured the boats and carried out spot checks to ensure compliance with the regulations. A popular spot for inspection was at the basin end of Nantwich aqueduct. Here, as boats came along the embankment, they were stopped — and the first thing inspected was usually the water can. This was required to hold not less than three gallons of fresh water and to be suitably painted on the inside to prevent rust. Len Wilson reports that the Shropshire Union looked after its fleet very well — and always had "change boats" ready to replace any craft likely to be found unsatisfactory. The Company also provided a number of wells along their route at which water cans could be replenished. These wells were not very deep. Square brick built structures, they just allowed a can to be dipped in. The well at Wheaton Aston was particularly unpopular with the boatmen because the water here was always covered with scum.

Life for the "Shroppie" boatmen deteriorated after 1921 as family boats became an economic necessity because the wife and children provided a "free" crew. The F.M.C. and Clayton oil boats which dominated the canal from the 1920's until the 1940's were classic examples of family boats. This was clearly brought home to Rolt during his encounter with a tar boat captain at The Wharf Inn, Cheswardine in 1939. This boatman's wife had recently died and her child of four had drowned in Tyrley top lock. Three children, the eldest a girl of ten, remained to help their father.

On these family boats the hardworking husband and wife ate, slept, lived and brought up children within the confines of a tiny cabin. This nomadic mode of life, was not of course without its social problems. Most boaters had no formal schooling and the landlord of the Wharf Inn thought it a scandal that many canalfolk were unable to tell the time from his clock. However illiterate many of these people were, by all reports they were certainly experts at counting money! Various attempts to remedy the educational problems of canal children were made — but to little real effect. A report to the Minister of Health made in 1921 recommended that canal children between the ages of four and fourteen should be prohibited from living on boats during term time — but it was never enforced. The same report went on to describe life on the boats of the day finding that "the presence of the wife and mother aboard helps to preserve a high standard of morality among the men and a kindly but efficient discipline among the children". That the canal people formed an almost forgotten section of the population is emphasised by the realisation by this Committee that "the Registrar General has no figures applicable to canal boat people". It had to be estimated that about 50% of canal children were being born on boats at about this time. All in all it is remarkable how well these canal families coped with their situation. Certainly they possessed an abundance of good humour, adaptability and determination.

Their floating homes all had much the same layout and built-in furniture. Table and beds folded up for the daytime, whilst much of the space was occupied by the range which provided heating and cooking facilities. Lighting was by candle or paraffin light. The lace plates, polished brasswork, and "roses and castles" decoration lent an air of charm and homeliness to the cramped environment. Women fulfilled vital tasks on the boats including washing, cooking, and child-minding while the men worked the boat. However, when motors appeared on the "Shroppie" the women were often given responsibility for the butty boat and spent long hours at the tiller. Even simple jobs like washing clothes were not easy on a narrow boat. Dirty canal water often had to be used while on the Clayton oil boats a makeshift washing line could be rigged up above their flat decks. The condition of narrowboats varied according to the occupants. Some were like floating slums but most families took great pride in their vessels which were as clean as new pins with the ropework immaculate and the boat's gunwales scrubbed clean. The lack of basic toilet facilities and running water on the boats inevitably made personal hygiene difficult. Despite such conditions the health of the boat people appears to have been generally good.

The outdoor life gave the crews keen appetites. In the nineteenth century boats only had simple stoves which meant that everything had to be boiled. Some boatmen virtually existed on "browiss" a popular poor man's meal. Pieces of bread were placed in a basin and mixed with pepper, salt, butter and Cheshire Cheese. Water was added and the ingredients then boiled to produce a thick kind of soup. By the First World War ranges with ovens had become widespread allowing the canalfolk to roast meat. Snacks were taken whenever possible and an endless supply of hot tea was always on hand. The main meal was taken in the evening when beef or mutton stews were popular but the odd hare, rabbit or pheasant provided a tasty change. Provisioning the boat was often done in a hurry at shops adjacent to the canal. Len Wilson remembers a bakers and general store at Gnosall Heath in Staffordshire which was much patronised by boaters. The shopkeeper, an old man known as Walwyn, was very kind to them, allowing a little credit and always serving the boatpeople immediately on entry,

The turn of the century and a scene of some confusion. Warps are being used to try and sort out the cluster of boats that has built up in the bridge hole. "Warrior", a Shropshire Union company boat, is laden with timber which has probably been imported via Ellesmere Port.

September 1959, with commercial carrying nearly at an end. An empty pair of British Waterways boats move north towards Nantwich, the crew of mother, father and son maintaining the traditions of family operated craft. The "rams head" rope work in the rudder stock and the painted water cans emphasise how little canal life changed over the years. The butty "Ipswich" was originally built for Fellows Morton and Clayton.

irrespective of the number of other customers waiting. Audlem was an equally convenient shopping place and in the 1920's it was a familiar sight to see all the "Shroppie" women folk hurrying to the nearby shops whilst the boats navigated the "thick" of locks. As the Audlem Scrapbook of 1951 comments, "The boat people are great meat eaters and the women were often to be seen in the past coming from the Audlem butchers with their white aprons laden with the best cuts".

Boatmen were forever needing to supplement their low wages and many became adept at poaching. For this their well trained dogs came in handy. Billy Skinner was a noted trainer and always kept two or three whippets on board for catching rabbits along the cut. The crack of a horse whip often disguised the blast of a shotgun, but other more devious ploys were used. For catching pheasants lengths of fishing line were run into a field or wood. Raisins, or other bait were placed on the fish-hooks which the unfortunate birds then swallowed.

The "Shroppie" runs through many important estates and the landowners were naturally suspicious of the boatmen. Near Brewood signs were erected warning boatmen of stiff fines for poaching, but a more effective deterrent were those keepers who frequently walked or cycled along the towpaths. On the northern "Shroppie" there was a close affinity between the poaching fraternity of Chester and the boatpeople. Gangs of men hitched regular lifts on narrowboats to Beeston in the evening and there spent the night on the local Peckforton Estate. They returned home hidden beneath the canvases of another boat early the next morning, safe with their night's haul and leaving the boat crew a rabbit or two the better off!

Although a rough honesty characterised the boat people — for they could be relied upon to respect and care for one another's property — a very different attitude existed towards the goods that they carried on their craft. In the same way as a pheasant or rabbit on a landowner's property was considered "fair game", so also was it with the cargoes. As one retired boatman gently put it "a lot of the food we carried on the boats was sampled by us!" When Len Wilson spent his month iced up at Audlem in 1917 the boat was carrying a load of flour and currants *en route* to a retail merchant in Smethwick. He re-calls that "during that freeze up our basic food was spotted dick!" Likewise Richard Jones remembers how a visit to Cadbury's factory at Knighton was looked upon as a bonus — for it provided an opportunity to stock up with fresh milk, rough chocolate and also sugar. As he was to learn on his first visit to the factory a certain amount of pilfering was expected. Before beginning to unload the twenty tons of sugar he was carrying a warehouseman approached. "Have you got any sugar?" he was asked. "Only on the boat" replied the young man. The warehouseman went to fetch a knife, slit open a sack and extracted a suitable ration of the sugar for the boatman! Cadbury's rarely counted the bags off the boats at Knighton where it became traditional that one such sack would always be left on the delivery boat — loosely covered over by one of the canvas "cloths". Tinned foods were also at risk. These were normally boxed in an attempt to minimise loss — but, with an expertise born of practice, the wooden lids would be sprung open and a few tins of pineapple or salmon or peas then removed. The contents would be consumed and the tins then refilled with soil or sand before being returned to the box!

Different cargoes would have their own private canal users names. Thus "Shroppie" boatmen would refer to sugar as "sand" and to Guinness as "nigger". Needless to say the tapping of a barrel of "nigger" stout was a popular pursuit, but one that took great skill. A chisel was used to ease out the bung from the side of the barrel. The Guinness was then siphoned out and was replaced by water. In this way the cargo was said to be "never short of weight, but only of quality"!

When commercial carrying ceased the canals lost more than just cargoes. A culture, little changed over a century and more, was also lost. The work of a boatman was hard and the long hours were poorly paid. The basic living conditions, lack of education and relative isolation bred a community that was private, shy and almost anachronistic. However it was an existence that brought its own satisfactions. Richard Jones — with memories stretching back to the earliest years of this century — is quite sure as to what he thought of life on the Shropshire Union. "It was the life I liked. You were always moving from one place to another, busy with the boat and locks, meeting people — and in the great outdoors".

VII : THE ROUTE DESCRIBED

The Wirral Line – Ellesmere Port to Chester

Not many canal journeys can start from a lighthouse nor from a museum – while even more rare are those that start with views of two cathedrals seen across an estuary....but the "Shroppie" manages to do all of these.

At **Ellesmere Port** the old river entrance of the dock area leads out to the Manchester Ship Canal on the one side – and into a tidal basin, once busy with Mersey traffic, on the other. A rise, through a single barge sized lock, brings one up into the dock estate proper. It was here in the nineteenth century that the growth and wealth of the town was established, and it is here today that one finds oneself in the heart of the **Boat Museum**.

For over a hundred and fifty years the area that grew from two linked locks and the junction with the River Mersey provided a focus for the canal. By the late 1960's it was derelict! Weeds and rubbish choked the locks, hulks lay rotting alongside derelict wharves, while by the end of 1970 even the lovely Telford winged warehouse had been destroyed – the result of neglect, vandalism and fire. But as the site was sinking into squalor and oblivion a group of five enthusiasts, concerned for the preservation of traditional canal craft, were looking for a location at which such boats could be restored and preserved. As a result of their efforts The Boat Museum was opened on its present site in June 1976 with a collection of just nine craft. From these beginnings the present day museum has emerged. Now, as the National Waterways Museum, it provides a unique and extensive combination of buildings, boats and associated equipment carefully restored and allowing the workings of this canal port to be re-created and brought back to life.

From **Bridge 147**, Powells Bridge, one can look back to the Museum area. The little lighthouse still guards the entrance to the Ship Canal and parallel broad and narrow gauge locks led upwards to the long pound of the Wirral Line. This then runs south and west, uninterrupted by any locks, down to Chester, nine miles away. The museum lies tucked into a gap between the Ship Canal and the Motorway. In front the Mersey stretches out – with Liverpool on the horizon, its skyline punctuated by the twin towers of the Anglican and Roman Catholic cathedrals. Away to the right, and north east across the river, the massive cooling towers of Fiddlers Ferry power station can also be seen. The canal, meanwhile, squeezes under the motorway to be swallowed up in the industrial wilderness it once helped to create.

Oil came to Ellesmere Port as long ago as 1870 when the Diamond Oil Company established itself and started to use the canal to carry its materials. With the coming of the Manchester Ship Canal, allowing deep water ships to come close to major market areas, oil storage development went ahead with rapid growth in the 1920's. Anglo-American Oil and Shell Mex built plants

In 1906 the Wolverhampton Corrugated Iron Company started production in Ellesmere Port, using steam powered barges on the northern broad sections of the canal. One of their steamers has just left the dock area and, passing moored narrow boats, moves south. The black and white "Canal Tavern" to the left has since been demolished.

in the area immediately to the east of the "Shroppie" at Stanlow — and the extensive activity that still goes on today leaves the heavy stench of petrochemicals in the air. As the canal creeps through the industrial fringe of the town this mingles with the smells of soaps and disinfectants from other works. After **Bridge 146** the waterway is crossed by the railway and immediately passes the backs of tall black corrugated warehouses. These were once the premises of the Wolverhampton Corrugated Iron Company whose boats and barges plied the canal in the early days of this century. The loading docks, where boats could be floated right into the factory premises, can still be seen. Slowly the town drops away. New piling protects banks where once rows of working boats tied up. The number of rings set into the old stone setts along this section show how busy this section of canal must once have been. Now it is the motorway that is busy, running parallel with the canal on a high embankment for some two miles beyond the museum. Past **Bridge 137** the tower of **Stoak** village church somes into view before the canal again passes under a flurry of motorway and older bridges. At last by **Bridge 135** gently undulating and undisturbed countryside is reached.

Caughall Bridge — **Bridge 134** — looks innocent enough today except perhaps that the newer cast iron section in the centre of the brick abutments suggest its life has not been entirely trouble free. Certainly it caused problems in 1821. A Company report of that year refers to repairs being necessary, adding that "many accidents have happened......on the Packet Boats" that then frequently used this section and that "lives have been lost....passing under bridges". The hillocks and humpy ground alongside the section that follows, cloak underground oil storage tanks, while between here and **Bridge 133** the occasional roar of a lion or howl of wolves confirms that **Chester Zoo** is near. The best route on foot from canal to Zoo is from Caughall Bridge — an easy walk of about a mile. The canal now passes through a shallow glaciated valley, the Backford Gap. Amid quietly pleasant countryside, and beneath **Bridge 131A**, a large sandstone viaduct carrying the Birkenhead railway north from Chester, the navigation starts to near the City.

With council estate and school to the right, from **Bridge 129** the squat Norman tower of Chester Cathedral can clearly be seen. On an embankment the town proper is entered — the distant hills of Wales away to the west. Backs of houses, red bricked and terraced, close in — until, under a roving bridge, the canal finally opens out into a basin. Here is **Tower Wharf**, the centre of the canal system in **Chester**. Immediately past the canal warehouse and workshops, the River Dee can be reached by branching right and immediately dropping down through three wide locks. It was access to this tidal river and the sea that encouraged the building of the original Chester Canal. Fitted into the triangle of land, between the canal and the locks to the Dee, is the ingenious covered dry dock of Taylor's boat yard. This can be filled by drawing water from the canal — and emptied by releasing its contents down into the river below. Here it was that the Shropshire Union Company built and maintained its own boats before eventually leasing the yard to the well known firm of J.H. Taylor in 1921. The wide and busy basin runs past the British Waterways Yard — at Tower Wharf itself — before the canal turns sharp left around a wide right angled bend, and up to the foot of the Northgate Locks and the Chester Canal.

The Chester Canal — Chester to Nantwich

Boats have been arriving at **Chester** for centuries. For the Romans it was an important port, remains of their harbour evident on the Roodee, the City race course. A massive section of their quay can still be found where the spectator stands come up to the unique city walls. These walls, built and modified over hundreds of years, but essentially medieval in their present form, run right around the city — an unbroken circuit of two miles. Gates punctuate these walls, and on the west the Watergate leads out to what was once the Roman harbour. A little further north is Water Tower and here it was, in May 1772, that the "Shroppie" really began. In March of that year the Act permitting the canal had been passed by Parliament. Two months later the Mayor, the subscribers, the engineers, lead by Samuel Weston, and twenty one workmen marched out to the strains of the Militia Band of Musick to "a field in the Quarry near the Water Tower....and there the Mayor cut the first sod of the canal".

NANTWICH TO ELLESMERE PORT

GRADIENT PROFILE

THE ELLESMERE CANAL

Chester to Ellesmere Port

9.5 miles   2 locks   14′- 11″ rise

1.57′ rise per mile

4.75 miles per lock

Bunbury Staircase Locks
2 // Fall 15′-7″
Tilstone Lock 9′- 8″
Beeston Stone Lock 8′- 6″
Beeston Iron Lock
7′- 0″
Wharton's Lock 7′- 8″
Christleton 9′-0″
Greenfield 9′-0″
Tarvin 8′-4″ Chemistry 8′-9″ Hoole Lane
3 // 32′ Chester Northgate Staircase
Whitby Locks
2 // 14′-11″
Sea Level
feet
140 120 100 80 60 40 20
28 26 24 22 20 18 16 14 12 10 8 6 4 2 0 miles
ELLESMERE PORT
CHESTER
BARBRIDGE JUNCTION
HURLESTON JUNCTION
NANTWICH
ELLESMERE CANAL
CHESTER CANAL

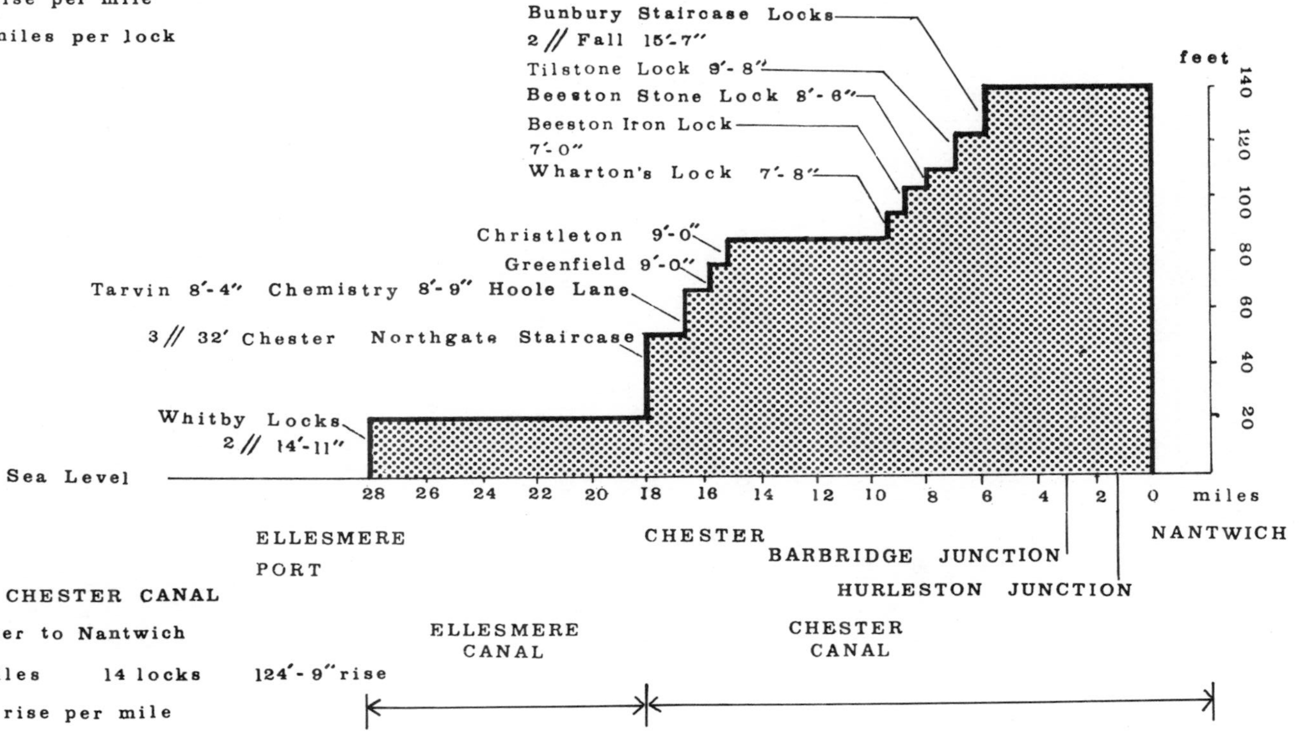

THE CHESTER CANAL

Chester to Nantwich

18 miles   14 locks   124′- 9″ rise

6.93′ rise per mile

1.28 miles per lock

The original route of the canal led straight down from **Northgate Locks** through five, rather than the present day three chambers, into the Dee. The bottom locks of the Northgate flight have since been abandoned and the sharp present day turn into the Tower Wharf basin with its separate locked route down to the Dee — provides the way to the river. Railway, road and canal all squeeze in under the shadow of the north west corner of the city walls. With trains clattering overhead on the old LMS main line and cars crossing the water to enter the city by St. Martin's Gate, the canal runs parallel with the walls to start its thirty two foot rise up through the wide staircase locks. The early days of the Chester canal were dogged by difficulty, but at least the impressive cutting running east-west along the side of the city walls provided one piece of good fortune. Where difficult excavation through sandstone had been expected it was found that the canal was following the route of an old Roman moat. The removal of accumulated soil, silt and debris was to prove far easier and cheaper than moving solid rock. However, unexpected problems cropped up on the section. The city gaol was situated at **Northgate** and the Canal Minute Book of July 1772 shows that "a proper method of securing the Prisoners confined in Northgate Gaol from making their escape during such time as the work shall be carried on" had to be agreed before the cut could be continued. High across this section the **Bridge of Sighs** spans the canal. The chapel for the gaol was situated outside the walls. Attempts to rescue condemned prisoners on their last journey to Chapel before execution became so common as to make the building of a separate bridge more easily controlled by the Sheriff and his men, an essential extension to the gaol. Even this was not enough — for high railings had then to be added to prevent the prisoners jumping over into the canal in a last desperate bid for freedom.

A turn takes the cutting around the north eastern angle of the walls. From the tower here, in September 1645, the dispirited Charles I is said to have watched the rout of his troops. Pushed back from the battle of nearby Rowton Heath by Parliamentary forces this defeat sealed the fate of Royalist Chester. The King fled while the City was left to face siege, starvation and eventual defeat. At **Cow Lane Bridge** the cutting gives way to a busy open urban scene. From here Frodsham Street, provides the best route into the City centre, while the canal moves quietly away into the industrial backdrops. On the right-hand bank Steam Mill Street comes up to the tow path. F.A. Frost & Sons originally had a flour mill on the River Dee but moved here to Steam Mill Street in 1817. Nearly 100 years later they were to move to Ellesmere Port to become one of the three large firms that helped regenerate the docks and the canal in the days immediately before the First World War.

Five locks, spaced at regular intervals over the next mile or so, gently lift the canal up to the main level of the Cheshire Plain. **Hoole Lane Lock** is on the edge of residential Chester where late Victorian and Edwardian

Cow Lane Bridge, Chester – with narrow boat "Sandbach" tied up alongside the timber yard where now stands the public house the "Lock Stock and Barrel". A Mersey flat can be glimpsed under the bridge to the right.

Trade Directories of the 1870s show B. T. Farrimond & Co. Timber Merchants, as importing Swedish timber to their Cow Lane Timber Yard. This would have been shipped via Ellesmere Port and brought down along the Wirral Line.

terraced houses slowly give way to larger properties. Immediately north of the canal runs the main railway line to Holyhead buried in a deep cutting with only the tops of signals showing above the banks. For many years "London Time" was taken from Euston to Dublin by this route, each night the guard of the "Irish Mail" being entrusted with carefully set watch for conveyance by train and boat to Ireland. This railway line follows the line of the canal closely, first past **Chemistry Lock** where any water by-passing the canal flows virtually under the lock-keepers cottage – and next past **Tarvin Road Lock** where an original round lengthman's hut may still be seen. Three of these huts still survive on the Chester Canal, the best preserved being further south at Tilstone. By **Greenfield Lock** the canal is in countryside. The top of a tall ex-L.M.S. signal post can just be glimpsed from the towpath before the railway disappears beneath the canal to emerge from a twin bore tunnel – but now on the south side of the cut. On this section, just before **Christleton Lock**, the tow path area widens and the remains of what appears to be a wide ditch can be traced. More careful inspection shows that this "ditch" was carefully built – a few remaining stone setts still marking its limits. When the railway company was working on the tunnel, just a few feet beneath the cut, it was necessary to divert canal traffic to this temporary alternative route so as to allow work on the railway to go ahead without risk of flooding.

Just before **Bridge 22** the neglected Christleton Mill, its elevator reaching out over the water, slips by. The village of Christleton is mainly set back from the canal but attractive gardens reach down to the waters edge while craft bob at their moorings. Christleton is a name of some significance in canal cruising history. It was from this village, in 1935, that G.F. Wain started to hire out motor cruisers for canal use and thus pioneered the hire-craft industry of today.

Quietly the canal moves deeper into rural Cheshire. At **Bridge 119** another waterside mill and more gardens reaching down to the water remind one that the village of Waverton is nearby. The original centre nestles beneath a sandstone church tower, a little way back from the canal — while away to the west the hills of Wales lie along the horizon. The rural tranquility is jolted a little at **Bridge 113**, for here a factory busy with the manufacture of agricultural land drains is sited alongside a rubbish tip — but in a matter of yards unspoilt country is reached again and the sandstone ridge of the mid-Cheshire hills begins to dominate the view ahead. Two castles perch on two facing crests. To the left, stands Beeston Castle perched on a rocky crag that rises abruptly for well over three hundred feet from the surrounding plain. The remains of the castle — built originally in 1220, but badly damaged during the Civil War — glowers from the top. Facing it from the right hand crest stands Peckforton Castle. At a glance this also seems old — yet it is some seventy years **younger** than the canal! Built in the late 1840's for Lord Tollemache it is but a replica of a gothic style castle. From these castles the hills slope away to the south — while the canal quietly continues its way on a route immediately to their north.

A small cluster of buildings — including Bates Mill complete with restored water wheel and mill pond — and the Shady Oak Inn — are passed at **Bridge 109**, after which the previously rather flat countryside through which the canal has been cut begins to gently undulate. By **Wharton's Lock** the first of five such upward steps in the space of some three miles is reached — and the route becomes rapidly more wooded. Virtually hidden in summer, deep among the rose bay willow herb and cow parsley that cram the copse to the right of the canal, a series of low embankments can be found — arranged as if to form a set of square shaped hollows. These puzzling structures are nothing more than a set of drainage pits, built to take canal dredgings, but never in fact, used. A little further along the route — and also along the course of the young River Gowy which runs parallel to the waterway through this section — a hint of menace intrudes. Tall speared metal railings guard an area of hillocks. Concrete paths and steps wind across their slopes while the blank windows of a metal shuttered house gaze down upon the canal. This is a strategic oil reserve. A few yards further on the railway embankment, with the tall Beeston and Tarporley signal box perched beside it, and the busy A49 crossing the water by **Bridge 107** bring an everyday normality back to the scene.

Beeston is a name that must have engraved itself upon the minds of the early canal proprietors. From the very beginning this section proved to be a problem — particularly so around the locks. The area is one of running sand — hard to persuade to lie on anything other than the shallowest slope, and proving an unstable and shifting base for any lock. Barely ten years after the canal was opened the lock at Beeston collapsed completely. In November 1787, without cash for repairs, Beeston was forced to become the temporary navigational limit of the canal. Various remedies were attempted, but it was not until new life and prospects were breathed into the whole Chester route first by the merger with the Ellesmere Company and then in 1826 by the passing of the Act for the Birmingham and Liverpool Junction section that serious attempts to solve the problem were made. Built on the advice of Telford, **Beeston Iron Lock**, a structure of iron plates bolted together and virtually impervious to the shifting sands around it, was completed in 1828. At the same time the short section up to **Beeston Stone Lock** was re-aligned a gentle curve skirting round the original route. The instability of the ground in this area still shows for the round lengthman's hut at the Stone Lock leans uncertainly away from the canal.

Almost immediately one of the prettiest sections of the "Shroppie" begins. Winding into trees a steep valley brings **Tilstone Bank Lock** into view. Here is yet another old water mill that was once fed by the River Gowy. The position of the mill pond can still be identified by the willows and alders that grow along what is now just a dry depression running along the tow path side of the canal. The last of the surviving round stone built lengthmen's huts stands by this lock in quite good condition with even the curved wooden door remaining. Between here and the next bridge at Bunbury the original canal took in its water from the reservoir on the slopes to the west at Bunbury Heath. But by 1782 the company was in such financial difficulties that it could not pay its debts to local landowners. Seeking retribution they drained the reservoir to bring traffic on the cut to an enforced halt.

Today there is rarely a shortage of water as it burbles and clatters through the large overflow running past the two staircased **Bunbury Locks**. These lift the canal 15'7" upwards towards Nantwich. On the one side, just below the spill weir taking water to the overflow, is the lock keepers cottage. On the other side are more of the former company buildings. A warehouse stands close to Bridge 105 — its gable end still carrying the legend "Shropshire Union Railways and Canal Company — Carriers" in large painted letters. Further along stands a long low building currently used for the construction of steel hulled boats. This once stabled company horses in twenty-two stalls. The smaller slate roofed building just below was a loose box believed to have been used for housing sick animals in isolation from the other stock.

Beyond these locks the countryside begins to flatten out as the Cheshire Plain re-establishes itself after the interruptions of the central ridge of sandstone hills. On the apex of the long curve leading up to **Bridge 104** a tumble of brick and masonry arches covered with soil butt up to the canal. These are the remains of what was once one of a number of

Barbridge circa 1925 with "Crane" – a narrow boat belonging to Griffiths, a firm of Chester millers – passing the Junction. Where now a large marina and moorings dominate the start of the branch, all then was quiet and empty.

brick works that clung to the canal in this area. Water proved an ideal carrying medium for the heavy raw materials and finished products involved and the simple wharf facilities that once existed can just be located among the canal side vegetation.

Under Bridge 104 — unusual for its storage of stop planks in its wing — and **Calveley** is reached. Through this little settlement run road, canal and railway together, all using the same low gap into the mid-Cheshire hills. Had the original intention of the Shropshire Union Company come to fruition it was from here that the railway south to Wolverhampton would have been built — making a junction with the old L.N.W.R. main line that has followed the canal down from Chester. In the event it became an important interchange site where goods were trans-shipped between boat and railway wagon. Two large concrete gate posts still stand showing where the connection between main line and sidings was made, while the flat cindered area beside the canal gives some idea of the extent of these once busy sidings. Passing extensive cheese warehouses that back onto the canal the waterway soon enters a short dull section running in a cutting beside the main Chester road. This crosses the canal by **Bridge 102**. On the opposite side to the road are the warehouses of North Western Farmers and other agricultural suppliers — incongrous beside them stands the large dish of a radio telescope. This is part of a small network of such telescopes all linked to a massive central telescope at nearby Jodrell Bank.

Almost immediately the canal reaches **Barbridge Junction** – once one of the busiest points on the Shropshire Union system. From here goods could be transhipped from boat to boat dependent upon their destination. The junction itself is made with the Middlewich branch, which goes off east under its own elegant winged bridge. This leads to the Potteries and Manchester. Further down the route, in little over a mile, lies Hurleston. From this the Llangollen branch leads off west into the once busy Welsh branches of the Company's waterways. Barbridge thus formed the virtual centre of a cross with canals running out from it in all four directions. A few remaining buildings, and the foundations of others still visible amongst the grass, show where previously warehouses and wharves clustered around the water at its narrowest point. Here, just south of the junction itself, an overall roof spanned the water – while at the end of the nineteenth century a mission hut for the boat people was also established on the site. Barbridge is still busy, but with commercial traffic that now rushes past on the main road parallel to the cut. Soon the bustle dies away as the canal curves back into quietly pastoral countryside on the short stretch to Hurleston.

Once under **Bridge 98** the tall grass covered banks that form the walls of Hurleston Reservoir dominate the view. Today this feeds the taps of South Cheshire rather than the canal – with water that has travelled down the branch from Llangollen. The branch survived plans made for its closure in 1944 when it was realised that the canal could be used as a ready made open pipe line. **Hurleston Junction** is reached immediately past the reservoir, the branch climbing away west to Wales up four closely sited locks. The main line lies straight ahead under **Bridge 97**, past an area used for dumping dredgings – before moving back into pastureland once more.

The original terminus of the canal is now less than two miles away in **Nantwich Basin**. En route from Hurleston the village of Acton, dominated by its red sandstone church tower, lies back from Bridge 93. Half a mile later, having passed the moorings of the Nantwich and Border Counties Yacht Club, the canal then forks. To the left, under the narrow gauge Bridge 92 lies the Birmingham and Liverpool Junction section to the Midlands. To the right the broad gauge section ends in Nantwich basin. Here the Chester canal arrived in 1779, first to struggle against lack of traffic and almost non-existent finance but later, on the completion of the full main line, to do steady trade in dairy, agricultural and other goods. From the wharves, now busy with pleasure craft, regular services to the whole of the kingdom were run for many years – while from the warehouse, now occupied by the British Waterways Board office, Cheshire Cheese was shipped to markets throughout the land.

The Birmingham & Liverpool Junction : Nantwich to Autherley Junction

On leaving the older Chester Canal, what originally was the route of the Birmingham and Liverpool Junction Canal is carried high on an embankment to the west of Nantwich. The distinctive tower of the parish church of St. Mary is a prominent landmark across the rooftops. The A51 Chester Road is crossed by a fine single-arched cast iron aqueduct, after which the canal swings round, leaving Dorfold Park on the right. Telford had planned to take the canal through the Park itself and directly into Nantwich Basin but the squire of Dorfold Hall objected and forced the building of the expensive and troublesome embankment to the east.

The first six miles along to Audlem generally lack interest as the canal cuts with a monotonous straightness through flat cattle-filled pastures. Momentarily the tranquillity of the scene may be shattered by a diesel train on the Crewe to Shrewsbury line which crosses the canal just south of Nantwich. It is hard to accept that a little over twenty years ago huge ex-L.M.S. Duchess and Royal Scot locomotives thundered along this route with their heavy South Wales expresses. **Hack Green Locks** soon break the boredom and an old stable block still survives in good repair. On the left the remnants of the old Great Western Railway route from Nantwich to Wellington appears and this keeps close proximity with the canal all the way to Market Drayton. Opened in 1863 the passenger services fell victim to Dr. Beeching a century later and complete closure followed in 1967. An interesting cast iron G.W.R. boundary post can be found on the towpath where the railway formerly crossed the canal.

A lofty embankment leads to the Moss Hall Aqueduct over the infant River Weaver. Not far away, under **Bridge 79**, comes the beginning of the famous **Audlem Locks**. This flight of fifteen locks lifts the canal up more than 90 feet in 1½ miles. Before the bottom lock the old canal stable block can hardly be missed — with its painted sign warning that it is "only for the use of Shropshire Union animals". When commercial traffic was busy on the canal, these stables were often full and in such a case boatmen would then have to take their horses to the Bridge Inn or the Combermere Arms in the village to find accommodation for them. **Audlem** has strong associations with the "Shroppie". In the days of working narrow-boats the boatwomen found it a convenient place to find time for shopping as the boats were navigated slowly through the many locks or "The Thick" as it was known in boat language. A link with the navvies who constructed the canal is provided by the grave of a man called Jackson in the local cemetery. Legend has it that he borrowed 2/6d (12½p) to buy his first spade and with this he then helped dig the cut! The local canalscape is still full of interest. The old Shropshire Union warehouse is now the "Shroppie Fly", a very popular hostelry, whilst Kingbur Mill has now been converted into an attractive canal craft shop. The centre of Audlem lies a short walk from the canal and is well worth exploring. The noble 15th century church of St. James the Great dominates the scene — surrounded by some interesting houses, shops, inns and the old butter market beneath.

Audlem lock flight looking down from Bridge 76 – circa 1900. The trees shown have now almost all been felled but otherwise the scene remains essentially the same. Note the drainage channel beside the well kept tow path.

South of Audlem, the rolling wooded countryside makes a welcome change from the relative monotony of the Cheshire Plain. The "Shroppie" passes half a mile to the east of the sleepy village of **Adderley** whose 19th century classical styled church can be seen in the distance. Here a group of five closely packed locks are kept in pristine condition with attractive flowerbeds and gravelled towpath fringing the water. **Bridge 14** signals the approach of Betton Woods where tradition has it that the old boatmen would never moor for the night — for fear of the shrieking ghost that haunts this section of the cut. Once away from this eerie gloom the abutments of yet another derelict railway bridge appear. This line was opened by the North Staffordshire Railway in 1870 and linked Market Drayton with the Potteries until the mid-1960's. The buildings of Drayton soon emerge on the skyline and the canal passes Victoria Wharf, the home of a long established coal merchant's business which was supplied by canal well into the 1940's.

Market Drayton is an important leisure boating centre with commercial operations by the "Ladyline Group" and "Holidays Afloat". The latter company utilise the old commercial wharves where a fine grain and general warehouse is the outstanding feature. In the decade before the outbreak of the Great War, William Rogers and Sons were the local grain merchants and their two boats, "Nellie" and "George", must have been familiar sights unloading here. The town centre lies some distance away from the canal;

it is graced by some fine buildings and a lively Wednesday market which perpetuates a 700 year old trading tradition.

Immediately south of Drayton the "Shroppie" crosses the Tern Valley by a lofty embankment fringed by pine trees. Westwards there are fine views towards the town with the imposing church of St. Mary's perched on a hill-top. Legend has it that Clive of India — who attended the local grammar school — once climbed the tower to sit on one of the gargoyles! A gloomy and narrow sandstone rock-cutting marks the beginning of an attractive flight of five locks at **Tyrley**. At the top, by Bridge 60 a delightful group of canal buildings congregate around the old wharf. As well as an attractive lock-keeper's house, there are also a warehouse and several cottages dated 1837 and 1840. These red-brick buildings were erected by the owners of nearby Peatswood Hall. Today they have been sympathetically restored and the end cottage is now a canal craftshop, its side wall the home to a poignant war memorial. A reminder of the canal's past history can be found on the roadbridge where there are two excellent Shropshire Union Railways and Canal Company cast-iron signs, warning would be users that "this bridge is insufficient to carry weights beyond the ordinary traffic of the district".

Once away from the bustle of Tyrley the famous **Woodseaves Cutting** is reached. Over a mile in length and ninety feet deep, William Provis, the contractor for this section, faced enormous difficulties here in 1829

Tyrley Locks circa 1900. The laden horse boat "Khartoum" approaches the flight, her helm dressed in the traditional boatwomen's garb.

AUTHERLEY JUNCTION TO NANTWICH

GRADIENT PROFILE

THE BIRMINGHAM & LIVERPOOL JUNCTION CANAL

Autherley Junction to Nantwich

39 miles   28 locks   176'-6" rise

4'-6" rise per mile   1 lock per 1.39 miles

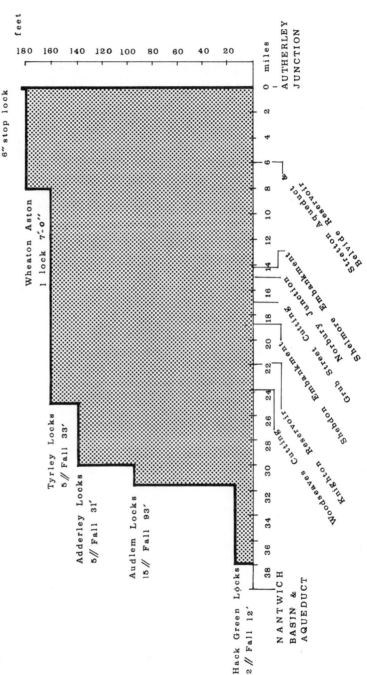

when trying to cut through the crumbling sandstone. To this day it provides plenty of work for British Waterways Board maintenance gangs, particularly so in winter when numerous landslips deposit red earth and rubble into the canal and onto the towpath. In this remote and inhospitable spot a pair of incredibly high and graceful bridges remain as a memorial to the canal builders. Although built only for farm accommodation purposes, their sandstone arches soar above the water and **Bridge 57** has gained fame as the much photographed "Rocket" or High Bridge.

After the semi-tropical atmosphere of Woodseaves it is a pleasant change to arrive at the old **Goldstone Wharf** and **Bridge 55**. In 1939 L.T.C. Rolt called here with "Cressy", his ex-Shroppie flyboat, and moored beyond the bridgehole in company with a Thomas Clayton tar-boat. A pleasant evening was spent in the secluded canalside inn. "We found", he wrote "a cheerful fire blazing in the little bar parlour, where sat the landlord, his wife and the captain of the horse-boat with a pint glass on the table before him". Today like many canalside pubs the Wharf Tavern has been modernised out of all recognition to cater for the influx of boaters during the summer. South of Goldstone the farmland is unspectacular but luxuriant. The red sandstone tower of St. Swithun's, Cheswardine is a prominent landmark but the most magnificent views are towards the hills of Shropshire to the west. No matter where you are in this part of the county, the whale shaped hill, the Wrekin, stands out as did the sandstone ridge and Beeston further north in Cheshire.

The canal cuts through Knighton Wood on another high embankment — or "valley" as the boatmen used to call them — and in so doing the canal enters Staffordshire. To the north lies Knighton Reservoir which formerly supplied the navigation with water. The hamlet of Knighton by **Bridge 45** is dominated by a large Cadbury's factory whose covered wharf still remains in excellent condition having been unused since the early 1960's. The plant now produces dried milk powder products where formerly it manufactured "chocolate crumb". One of the last working boats to serve Knighton was the British Waterways Board's "Mendip" — fortunately still preserved. In the 1950's "Mendip" was operated by Charlie Atkins who became something of a local celebrity in canal circles — and was nicknamed "Chocolate Charlie". He lived on "Mendip" until his death in the winter of 1981-82.

Shebdon Great Bank carries the canal southwards from Knighton for over a mile, towering sixty feet above the surrounding fields. At **Shebdon Wharf** the Newport to Adbaston road tunnels under the canal while nearby is the Wharf Inn, yet another canalside pub with which the "Shroppie" seems well supplied. At **Bridge 42** near the hill top village of High Offley, stands the isolated Anchor Inn with its sadly derelict stable block which was formerly a popular mooring for horse-boats. The pub started life in the 1830's as the New Inn but in the 1850's it became known as the Sebastopol in commemoration of the famous Crimean War battle. From 1906 until the 1960's the boat people were served by Mrs. Lily Pascall who was often woken up in the early hours by bargees banging on the doors and demanding ale! Today the Anchor remains one of the most traditional canalside pubs in the country with its wooden settles, window shutters and beers brought up from the cellar glass by glass.

The infamous **Grub Street Cutting** begins at **Lambarts Bridge No. 41.** A mile long and eighty feet deep, persistent rock falls made this cutting another headache for the builders who were forced to drastically open it out to minimise landslips. The dampness encourages trees, bushes and creepers to prosper and in the eeriness it is easy to believe in the boat people's ghost stories. The A519 Newport to Eccleshall road crosses Grub Street on the famous **High Bridge No. 39** which has an unusual strengthening arch which supports a 'iny telegraph pole.

Norbury Junction is a classic example of a self-contained canal community which grew up alongside the Birmingham and Liverpool in the

Norbury Junction circa 1905. The Shropshire Union boat "Penguin" is moored alongside the Company yard, while another narrow boat has been hauled out onto the bank beyond. A tub boat from the Shropshire Canal system can also be seen in the middle distance.

1830's. Until 1944 it boasted a junction with the Newport Branch which gave access to the Shrewsbury Canal and the tub-boat system of waterways serving the collieries, ironworks and quarries of Donnington and Coalbrookdale. Before nationalisation Norbury was the southern headquarters of the Shropshire Union and this importance has been perpetuated. The British Waterways Board Section Office, which supervises canal maintenance from Autherley to Audlem, is based here. The old workshop buildings, canal cottages and attractively whitewashed roving bridge over the defunct Newport arm lend an air of timelessness to the scene. Gone, however, are the working narrowboats whose crews flocked to the old Junction Inn to drink and brawl. Locals can also remember occasions in the 1920's and 1930's when the canal was frozen over and trapped narrowboats stretched far away into the chilled and foggy distance. Today Norbury Junction survives as a flourishing canal centre. The important hire fleet of Shropshire Union Cruisers is based here and the horsedrawn narrowboat "Iona" plies this section in the summer.

Norbury marks the northern end of the mile long **Shelmore Embankment**. Six years of toil by six hundred navvies were needed before this embankment was finally complete. Trees and vegetation today disguise the true height of the "Great Bank" but when new the earthworks must have been a stark and uncompromising scar on the landscape. Had Lord Anson of Norbury Park not insisted on the canal making a detour to avoid his prized game reserves, Shelmore would have been unnecessary!

On the outskirts of Gnosall the canal tunnels under a large bridge which until 1964 carried passenger trains from Stafford to Wellington. Opened in 1849, it has an interesting relationship with the canal because this was the one railway built by the "Shropshire Union Railways and Canal Company" during its courtship with railway conversion during the 1840's. At **Bridge 36** the "Shroppie" reaches the canalside settlement of Gnosall Heath. The A518 Newport to Stafford road crosses the canal and here are two distinctive buildings, the Navigation Inn and the former Coton steam-powered flour mill, now in use as a canal shop. Len Wilson who worked on the "Shroppie" from 1913 - 1945 remembers the mill as a bakery and general store. The owner being sympathetic to the boatpeople often let them have goods "on the slate". A few hundred yards further on is the interesting Boat Inn which with its curved wall matches the abutments of **Bridge 34.**

Cowley Tunnel has the distinction of being the only one on the Shropshire Union main line. Wide and impressive, its 81 yards of unlined sandstone lead into a spectacular deep and narrow defile – beautifully clad with trees, mosses and ferns. In summer a tropical gloom pervades, and the rays of sun which pierce the leaves and branches cast interesting patterns on the water and rock below. Cowley Cutting gives way to quiet unspoilt grazing land frequented by herons and kingfishers. Close to **Bridge 25** is the old High Onn Wharf which served the nearby village of

Church Eaton. Sandstone blocks indicate where long departed narrow boats moored, the scene dominated by a magnificent two-storey red-brick warehouse. In the vicinity of Little Onn the canal plunges into yet another wooded cutting known as Rye Hill, near to which lies the remains of an old wartime aerodrome.

The straggling village of Wheaton Aston is the next settlement on the banks of the "Shroppie". The Hartley Arms Inn lies along side **Bridge 19** and a short distance away is the lock which marks the end of the long unbroken seventeen mile pound from Tyrley. A depressing sight here is the derelict lock keeper's cottage built out of distinctive industrial blue brick. This spot was the scene for a wartime incident which locals remember well. A F.M.C. narrowboat bound for the Midlands with a cargo of uncovered aluminium on a bright moonlit night was observed by a German bomber. In the ensuing attack bombs were dropped which landed into a field only a hundred yards from the lock!

Lapley Wood Cutting is a particularly attractive and peaceful stretch of waterway which lies three quarters of a mile to the west of the village from which it takes its name. The variety of trees and wildflowers enhances its appearance in summer and provide a fitting approach to the famous **Stretton Aqueduct** which crosses the London to Holyhead road, — itself reconstructed under Telford's supervision in the 1830's. The aqueduct consists of a sturdy but elegant cast-iron trough which bears the inscription "Birmingham and Liverpool Canal, Thomas Telford. F.R.S.L. and E. Engineer 1832". The ironwork is well complemented by the blue-brick abutments and decorative sandstone columns. Immediately upon leaving the A5, the massive headbanks of **Belvide Reservoir** rear up on the right and a feeder from this can be seen entering the canal. Built in the 1830's to supply water to the canal, it is now being developed as a nature reserve under the auspices of the Royal Society for the Protection of Birds.

The quiet but charming village of **Brewood** sees little of the canal which hides away in a bold cutting. The former wharf has been tastefully converted into a boatyard by Countrywide Cruisers and this is only a short distance from the high and impressive **Bridge 14** which gives access to the village centre. The Boat Inn, with its fine sign, looks across the canal to St. Mary's Roman Catholic Church. At School Bridge the cutting gives way to an embankment which at last opens up a fine prospect of the village with its attractive Georgian houses dominated by the imposing steeple of the thirteenth century parish church. **Bridge 11** has the curious name of Giffard's Cross, for nearby it is reputed that in 1513 Sir John Giffard shot an escaped wild panther with a crossbow, thus saving the lives of a woman and her child! The classical balustraded **Avenue Bridge No. 10** spans another deep cutting and its abandonment of the canal's functional architecture allows it to blend in with the surroundings. This ornate sandstone structure was built upon the insistence of the Giffards whose tree lined avenue to Chillington Hall was pierced by the canal. Nearby a cast iron milestone proclaims that it is only 4 miles to Autherley Junction and the end

The ornate Avenue Bridge (No. 10) built to placate the Giffard family of nearby Chillington Hall. The canal cuts through the avenue of trees leading up to the Hall – hence the need for a bridge of appropriate elegance and style. This view – taken about 1930 – shows the canal in excellent condition despite the abandonment of Company carrying a few years earlier.

of the Birmingham and Liverpool. The canal continues on a direct passage through a landscape of fields which roll away into the distance punctuated here and there by isolated farmhouses. **Bridge 8** is approached by a deep narrow cutting for two hundred and fifty yards which provides little room for passing. There are two other similar rock cuttings in the next few miles to Pendeford. Old boatmen well remember heated disputes between narrowboat masters on these narrow sections. When no-one would give way, large groups of boats built up on either side of the arguing and heated blockage. Between **Bridges 5 and 6** the M54 Telford Motorway is an emphatic reminder that motor transport was a prime cause of the canal's decline after the First World War.

The pastoral landscape so characteristic of the "Shroppie" terminates abruptly at **Bridge 4**. The large factory of Dowty, Boulton and Paul manufactures aviation and defence equipment and in the Second World War was the birthplace of the unsuccessful Defiant fighter. Built with a heavy gun turret, this aircraft proved too slow for convential fighter use – but eventually found a role as a night fighter. The aircraft factory was a target for the Luftwaffe one Sunday evening in 1940 but the bombs narrowly missed and hit the canal instead. The final mile to Autherley passes through newly built housing estates, where attempts to landscape the canal banks are to be applauded. In the midst of this modern urban environment, **Bridges 2 and 3** seem strangely out of place, but are nevertheless useful vantage points for panoramic views of Wolverhampton. To the left the summit of Bushbury Hill is crowned by a distinctive clump of trees, whilst the chimneys of "Goodyear's" tyre factory stand tall and unmistakeable. In the midst of office blocks of the town centre stands the parish church of St. Peter which survives as a reminder of Wolverhampton's former importance in the wool trade.

At **Autherley Junction** the Birmingham and Liverpool joins the "Staffordshire and Worcestershire", a much older Brindley designed canal which opened in 1772. Where once was just fields — and later canals — now is unattractive urban growth and a sewage works. Even amidst this drabness there are reminders that this was once a busy and important canal junction. The two stable blocks with their distinctive roof ventilators are now used by "Water Travel" and the Wolverhampton Boat Club, whilst whitewashed canal cottages and a lock-keeper's house lend further character to the scene. An interesting survival of inter-company jealousies is the stop-look dividing the two waterways with a fall of only 6 inches. This was put in at the insistence of the Staffordshire and Worcestershire company who feared that the new canal would steal their water! At the lockside is the old office where boatmen would pay a toll according to the weight of cargo in their narrowboat's hold. For many years it was manned by the legendary Sam Lomas who worked here until shortly before his death in 1970. On a summer's day Autherley is thronged with pleasure cruisers but the surviving tollbooks reveal that forty years ago it was busy with a different type of traffic. On 6th March, 1943, for example, the Fellows, Morton and Clayton motor boat "Columbia" passed through with 21 tons of flour, bound for Wolverhampton. She was charged a toll of £2-0-3d. (£2.1½p). For over 130 years such working narrowboats were the life blood of Autherley Junction which boasted neither warehouses, nor proper road access and was even unknown to most Wolverhampton people. But to the "Shroppie" boatmen it was "Cut End" — part of their way of life and a canal junction which was the gateway to the industrial Midlands.

"The Middlewich Branch" – Middlewich to Barbridge

From the main line at Barbridge the Middlewich branch leads off east on its ten mile journey to join with the Trent and Mersey canal. Drifting across the quiet dairylands of central Cheshire it is easy to forget that this short arm of the Shropshire Union System, although among the first of its sections to be planned was almost the last to be built. A victim of inter-company rivalry from the very outset it was not able to fulfil its true potential as a busy cargo carrying canal until the railways had made this almost too late.

At **Middlewich** the branch leaves the Trent and Mersey on the south eastern fringe of the undistinguished town. Immediately it passes under Bridge 168 – elegantly inscribed "Wardle Canal 1829". This consists of just a few yards of cut up to a single lock – yet through this all the traffic had to pass and in doing so was forced to pay heavy compensation tolls. The branch (still locally known as "The New Cut") was opened throughout in September 1833. Repeated attempts to by-pass the short Wardle Canal section were legally blocked by the Trent and Mersey faction – and not until 1888 were the tolls finally lifted. The original plans for a Chester Canal running unimpeded through to Middlewich and the rich salt and pottery traffic date back to 1772. Yet over a hundred years were needed before these plans came to fruition.

Once away from the Trent and Mersey the canal immediately starts on its climb towards this main line. A well maintained cottage presides over the lock, and it is at the head of this that the Middlewich branch proper begins. The canal swings west through the suburban edge of the town, onto an embankment to cross the River Wheelock – and out to countryside beyond. The deep **Stanthorne Lock** next lifts the canal sharply upwards onto the six mile pound that provides the longest unbroken stretch of water on the branch. Over the main line of the Shropshire Union the average rise per lock is little more than 7 feet – but the three locks of the Middlewich branch are all of 11 feet or more.

Cheshire is still a largely agricultural county. The next few miles provide plenty of evidence of this. Substantial black and white half timbered farm houses are matched by the black and white Friesian dairy cattle that graze these productive grasslands. Equally substantial 19th century farm buildings show how this part of the country grew wealthy feeding the growing industrial populations of Manchester and the North West. Within a few years of the completion of the canal the same industrial and commercial pressures were providing the driving force for the coming railway age. A mere four years after the completion of the canal it was to be crossed by the Grand Junction Railway. By 1837 Robert Stephenson and Joseph Locke had jointly surveyed and built the line, and **Bridge 22A** carries this railway, the main west coast route to the North, across the canal. Heavily grooved rubbing stakes beneath the bridge show how for years these two very different transport systems co-existed in this otherwise quiet and almost forgotten corner of Cheshire.

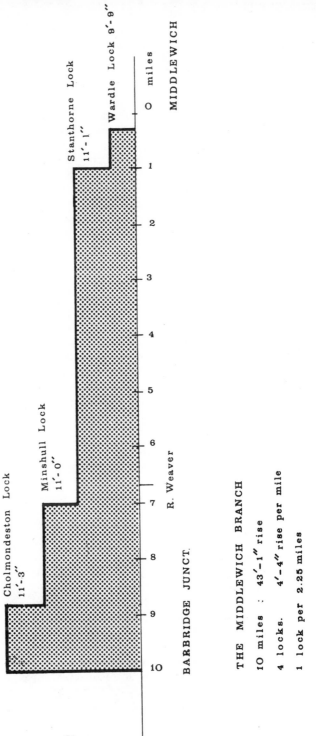

MIDDLEWICH BRANCH

MIDDLEWICH TO BARBRIDGE JUNCTION

GRADIENT PROFILE

Cholmondeston Lock
11'-3"

Minshull Lock
11'-0"

Stanthorne Lock
11'-1"

Wardle Lock 9'-9"

BARBRIDGE JUNCT.

R. Weaver

MIDDLEWICH

0 miles

THE MIDDLEWICH BRANCH

10 miles : 43'-1" rise

4 locks.   4'-4" rise per mile

1 lock per 2.25 miles

The branch winds gently on, following the side of a low hill below which the waters of Winsford Flashes sparkle into view. These wide lake-like sections of the River Weaver are the upper boating limits of this still important river navigation. The canalised river flows away north through the town of Winsford — just visible from the canal itself — to pass the one active English salt mine at Winsford — before reaching the River Mersey at Runcorn on its journey towards the sea. The winding upper reaches of the Weaver run roughly parallel to the Middlewich branch as it continues its curving course to the west. A few yards from **Bridge 18** a tall disused house and an associated range of buildings are to be found. This is the derelict stable block that once housed the company horses that worked this section of the canal. Extensions to the stables were made in 1898 — evidence of the increase in traffic that followed from the lifting of the tolls.

Gently curving, the canal continues to wind its way through the undulations of rural Cheshire — in doing so following the flank of a low hill. From **Bridge 14** — graced by a nearby house with elegant Dutch gables — the road runs down to the small village of Church Minshull. It was here that L.T.C. Rolt, during his classic canal journey as recorded in "Narrow Boat", paused for a "prolonged stay". When he came here in the closing years of the 1930's, with war drawing closer by the day, he found the village as a microcosm of an older England. The early 18th century church, the "Old Badger" inn and the farm are all still here — as are the black and white half timbered buildings of this little settlement....but the cattle food is now housed in a tall modern silo and the mill, that once generated local electricity as well as grinding grain, now lies forgotten and forlorn. Once the River Weaver powered this mill — but now it just tumbles past, soon to be crossed by the canal.

Beyond **Bridge 10** the branch moves onto a steep embankment, the sandy meandering banks of the river well below. Through large brick portals, with overflow tunnels on either side, the Weaver burrows for more than 50 yards beneath this embankment and the canal. To scramble down to river level and explore the overflow tunnels — which are entirely dry except during flood conditions — is well worth the effort involved.

The metal gates of **Minshull Lock** soon provide an 11 foot step upwards towards the Cheshire Plain, then beyond **Bridge 6** the canal runs ruler straight for almost exactly a mile. It was on this section that the locomotive towing experiments of 1888 took place. The idea is believed to have been that of the autocratic F.W. Webb — who for more than 30 years was Chief Mechanical Engineer to the extensive L.N.W.R. railway empire. A mile of 18" narrow gauge railway track was laid along the tow-path between Bridges 5 and 6 and a small 0-4-0 locomotive named "Dickie" brought out from the nearby Crewe Works. Up to six boats at a time could be hauled and at speeds of up to seven m.p.h. A major practical problem emerged. It was found very difficult to keep the leading boat of a string from being pulled in towards the bank — although officially the experiment was

The steam haulage experiment of 1888. The 18 inch narrow gauge railway line was laid on the straight section between Bridges 5 and 6 on the Middlewich branch. F. W. Webb, the L.N.W.R. Chief Mechanical Engineer, resplendent in top hat, looks on as the little locomotive "Dickie" brought from Crewe Works tugs away. The problem of keeping boats out from the bank can be clearly seen. In the centre of the picture a long pole is being used in an attempt to solve the problem. Materials for the experiment were brought to the site along the main Holyhead railway line just visible on the embankment beyond.

abandoned due to the high cost of laying track along tow paths. The horse was thus left unchallenged as motive power for the main Company fleet.

Bridge 5 carries the main Holyhead railway line across the canal which almost immediately reaches **Cholmondeston Lock**. With a rise of 11'3" this is the highest of any single lock on the whole Shropshire Union system. The countryside around is rather flat and dull — while on a low embankment the canal moves towards the nearby junction with the main line. After **Bridge 2** extensive moorings begin that continue until **Bridge 1**. Here, with traffic rushing past on the main road ahead, **Barbridge Junction**, with its remnants of what was once a busy interchange site, comes into view.

VIII : THE "SHROPPIE" TODAY

For some one hundred and fifty years boats have been travelling the length of the Shropshire Union main line. From Autherley Junction to Ellesmere Port the waterway falls for more than three hundred feet down forty four locks. Each boat travelling northwards to the sea will use at least one lock full of water, between 25,000 and 30,000 gallons being the typical capacity of the narrow gauge locks found between the Black Country and Nantwich – while the locks on the broad gauge sections through to Chester and Ellesmere Port require nearly 60,000 gallons for the passage of a boat. The "Shroppie", as with all other working canals, has been using a lot of water for a very long time.

The earliest days of the route saw the crucial water supply being drawn from the now almost forgotten reservoir at Bunbury Heath, but with the opening of the Birmingham and Liverpool Junction in 1835 the bulk of the water used was to come from the reservoirs on the newer southern section – the gradient of the "Shroppie" lying all in one direction, downhill from Birmingham to the sea.

Of these reservoirs the Belvide, just south of Wheaton Aston, served as the principal source of water. A second reservoir on the southern section was also built at Knighton. However, in recent years, the main water supply for the "Shroppie" has come from the very head of the canal itself, at Autherley Junction. Here in the earliest days of the Shropshire Union, its neighbour, the older Staffordshire and Worcestershire Canal was concerned to protect its own water fearing that every boat entering the "Shroppie" would take with it a lock full of the Staffs. and Worcs.! For this reason a stop lock, with a drop of a mere 6 inches, is encountered at the southern entrance to the canal. This was built to ensure that a boat entering or leaving the "Shroppie" would only deprive its neighbour of the very minimum of water! Now jointly controlled by the British Waterways Board the question of water ownership no longer applies, nor is there any shortage of supply at the Junction – for, since 1958, the adjacent Barnhurst sewage works has been putting up to 12 million gallons of purified effluent into the canal per day. It is this water that now supplies the major "Shroppie" requirements for most of its length. Belvide Reservoir still contains some water – but with weakened banks it is only safe for a reduced capacity. It mainly serves as a nature reserve and bird sanctuary, some club fishing also being allowed. Further north the reservoir at Knighton has been entirely de-watered. Earth movements in the 1950's made it unfit for use while the newly aquired supply of water from Barnhurst removed the need for its repair. The third major reservoir on the "Shroppie" is still in good condition and still in use – but primarily for the supply of drinking water rather than for the canal. Dating back to the first years of the nineteenth century Hurleston Reservoir was built at the same time as the Llangollen branch. Originating on the Welsh River Dee, up to 6 million gallons a day flow down the branch. Much goes into the reservoir itself to be purified and piped away, while the remainder helps feed the northern section of the main line.

Along the length of the canal natural drainage adds to the water supply. Much of this enters by field drains, while "run-off" along the many miles of its banks adds to the brown waters of the "Shroppie". In the wider slower sections silt settles and builds up on the bed of the canal while in the narrower sections the faster flow of the water leads to less sedimentation as a flushing effect is produced which keeps the water course relatively clear. Telford's plans for the southern part of the route show an envisaged water depth of 5 feet across the central half of a given 30 feet cross section. Despite the regular dredging of those lengths known to have a particular tendency to siltation, it is doubtful if the "Shroppie" is as deep as this anywhere today. With the demise of commercial traffic the depth of water once needed by a narrow boat, heavily loaded and down to its gunwales, is no longer required — while even from the earliest days of this century the canal was well known as being particularly shallow.

Although shallow the Shropshire Union has a long standing reputation for being a well maintained canal. The legacy of care and attention left by the old Company is being continued. British Waterways Board depots at Chester and at Norbury Junction care for the northern and southern halves respectively. The total staff is only a fraction of what it has been. In its heyday the Norbury base employed one hundred and twenty men. However, mechanisation has in part made up for the loss of man power. Dredging has been almost completely mechanised while if the clay puddling on a section needs repair it is the arm of a mechanical digger rather than many muddy boots that will tramp down the new lining. In an era of restricted finance maintenance priorities must be towards the canal itself. As a result much tow-path mileage has suffered badly from comparative neglect. Agricultural gangs cut hedges, re-fence, lop or fell dangerous trees and clear the culverts. They also do what they can for the paths, but in particular where the money and labour to renew the essential drainage beneath tow-paths is lacking, severe deterioration has set in. This is particularly noticeable in the deep cuttings south of Market Drayton. Telford's plans show tow-paths of 10 feet wide, while photographs taken before the First World War provide evidence that tow paths of this width were retained in excellent condition, even through the dampest and narrowest sections. Today's walker can only slip and stumble along their muddied and narrowing remains. On most of the route however the paths are in fairly good condition — albeit for walkers but not for horses.

Deterioration set in during the 1920's. The horse drawn fleet of the Shropshire Union Company disbanded, the main line was increasingly used by motor boats. The wash that these created rapidly caused erosion and subsequent silting problems that continue up to the present day. By far the largest single maintenance expense now incurred is that for bank protection. The "Shroppie" needs particular attention in this respect for with its many high embankments severe and widespread flood damage can be caused by breaching. Serious post-war breachings have included those at Cheswardine in 1952, in 1957 at High Onn and Adderley — and again at Adderley in 1963. A serious breach also occured at Church Minshull in 1958.

When regularly used and adequately maintained canals wear well. Bridges and locks — with original stone and brick work going back over a century and a half — abound on the "Shroppie". Lock gates, however, need regular replacement, typically at intervals of between fifty to seventy years. In the 1970's, as part of an attempt to reduce maintenance costs, a number of steel gates were installed on both the main line and on the Middlewich branch. However, it has since been found that steel needs **more** rather than less maintenance than wood — the need for regular painting adding to its costs. As a result all new "Shroppie" lock gates are again being built of wood. They are made in Cheshire at the main B.W.B. depot at Northwich — each gate being individually built to the particular measurements of the lock being repaired.

The "Shroppie" was built as a carrying route, yet, despite being without commercial traffic it is busier today than ever before. The well known boatman Jack Tolley worked for many years on the main line — his British Waterway's Admiral class motor boat "Mountbatten" carrying the occasional pay load even into the early 1970's. He remembers when a passage through the fifteen locks at Audlem would take as little as two hours. On a busy summer Saturday it can now take over five hours to rise or fall the ninety three feet of the flight.

Among those watching the holiday makers' boats take turns to enter and leave the locks will be those who choose to walk and stroll along the tow path. In the intensely farmed counties of Shropshire and Cheshire the canal paths of the old Shropshire Union provide an increasingly important means of access to the countryside. Once the Company would close its paths for a day each year, so as to retain legal control over access — but today the British Waterways Board, working in co-operation with the Countryside Commission, is aware of the recreational value of these paths, and most of those on the Shropshire Union are now public rights of way.

In the coarse fishing season these paths also provide for the needs of anglers. On many weekends rows of green fishing umbrellas, protruding rods and the earnest statuesque figures of fishermen perched on the bankside proclaim that another competition is taking place — while solitary or grouped anglers belonging to the various clubs with fishing rights on the waterway likewise try their luck or skill. The Shropshire Union is a good fishing canal and offers a wide range of coarse fish species — in particular bream and roach. From Ellesmere Port to Knighton, and also along the Middlewich branch, fifty six miles of fishing rights are held by the Shropshire Union Angling Association. This unique consortium — currently made up of five clubs — draws its membership from a wide area across the North West Midlands. South of Knighton half a dozen other clubs have rights on shorter lengths. Holiday makers on cruising craft also fish the "Shroppie" having first obtained weekly "Fishing from Craft" Permits issued by the British Waterways Board.

But the canal was built for boats — and craft by their hundreds still use it. In the mid 1930's the earliest canal hire cruises appeared on the waterway, but it was not until the demise of commercial carrying that the present hire craft business really got under way. Hulls, suitable for conversion to cruising use, became steadily available during the 1950's and this coincided with a gathering interest in waterways restoration and recreation. There are now ten major hire firms on the Shropshire Union main line, including the British Waterways Board who established their own hire base at Nantwich in 1958. Privately owned cruisers also abound on the "Shroppie". It provides access to some of the best inland cruising waters in the country including the Llangollen branch and the Cheshire Ring. Club moorings at Nantwich and Autherley Junction, private moorings at Hargrave and Stoke — and the extensive pontoon moorings at the large marina near Barbridge Junction all testify to the great popularity of the Shropshire Union.

However, survivors of the once huge Company fleet have now almost completely gone. The Boat Museum at Ellesmere Port provides many examples of the craft that once worked this waterway. Representatives of the Mersey flats, the Fellows Morton and Clayton and the Thomas Clayton tar boat fleets — as well as the more recent British Waterways craft that once plied the main line, are all exhibited. But one must look out for a hotel boat if one wants to see the unique sight of a Shropshire Fly still at work on its native waters. "Saturn" was built in the traditional materials of oak and elm, back in 1906, by the Shropshire Union Carrying Company at its Chester yard. For many years she collected cheeses from the dairy farms along the main line then running them up the Middlewich branch for sale in Manchester. Now owned by Inland Waterway Holiday Cruises she has been fitted out as a hotel boat, and as butty to her motor "Jupiter" she carries passengers over the whole canal system.

Whether as walkers, fishermen or boaters, all those who come into contact with the "Shroppie" are part of the paradox that our waterways provide. Canals were an essential part of the Industrial Revolution yet they offer us with a peaceful escape from so many of its consequences. The construction of the Shropshire Union spanned the central years of the canal age. Its oldest section, the Chester Canal, was an early response to the transport needs generated by increasing industrialisation. Its final miles, built with such great difficulty between Nantwich and Autherley Junction, were constructed in the shadows of the advancing railway age. As such its foundations are firmly fixed in a world of industrial endeavour and commercial competition. The clatter of the manufactures of the Black Country and the hustle and bustle of the wharves at Ellesmere Port were linked by this long quiet stretch of water. For well over a century the main line, the Middlewich branch and the other parts of the Shropshire Union system served their original purpose. A period of relative neglect and under use was then to follow — but now, with the focus on tranquillity and recreation, the "Shroppie" has come back into its own.

The management may change but the "Shroppie" goes on. Two notices on Bridge 60 by Tyrley Wharf.

ACKNOWLEDGEMENTS

The authors and publishers wish to thank the following for permission to reproduce illustrations on the pages indicated:

The Boat Museum, Ellesmere Port. 17, 19, 23, 40, 44, 48, 51, 66, 72.

Cadbury Brothers Limited. 28, 43.

D. L. McDougall. 14, 37, 55, 69.

The National Railway Museum, York. 20, 65.

E. W. Paget-Tomlinson. 52.

J. G. Parkinson. 32.

Shrewsbury Local Studies Library. 4.

Stafford County Record Office. 10, 34.

Harry Theobald collection. 47.

M. E. Ware. 77.

The Waterways Museum, Stoke-Bruerne. 13, 25, 31, 62.

In addition to the published sources identified much personal help, advice and information had been generously provided. In particular our thanks are due to Mr. Len Wilson and Mr. Richard Jones – both former employees of the Shropshire Union Railways and Canal Carrying Company – as well as to Mr. Tony Hirst and his staff at the Boat Museum; Mr. R. A. Jamieson of the Waterways Museum, Stoke-Bruerne; Mr. R. Jones, B.W.B. Northwich; Mr. G. Cliff; Dr. David Owen; Mr. E. W. Paget-Tomlinson; Miss R. M. Pearce and Mr. K. Robinson.

BIBLIOGRAPHY

As well as the wide range of journals, maps and company records consulted the following publications have proved particularly useful:

Aspinall P. and Hudson D., Ellesmere Port – The Making of an Industrial Borough (1982).

Cubbon T. W. Only a Little Cockboat (1928)

Donaldson-Hudson R. – The Parish of Cheswardine (1939)

Faulkner A. H. – Claytons of Oldbury (1978)
     F.M.C. (Fellows Morton and Clayton) (1975)

Hadfield C. – Canals of the West Midlands (1967) 2nd Edition

Jarvis A. – Ellesmere Port – Canal Town (1977)

Owen D. E. Cheshire's Waterways (1979)

Paget-Tomlinson E. W. – Canal and River Navigations (1979)
     Britain's Canal and River Craft (1979)

Priestley J. – Navigable Rivers and Canals (1831) Re-printed

Richards E. – The Leviathan of Wealth. The Sutherland Fortune
    in the Industrial Revolution (1973)

Rolt L. T. C. – Narrow Boat (1948)
    Thomas Telford (1958)

de Salis H. – Bradshaw's Canals and Navigable Rivers (1904) Re-printed

Seymour J. – Voyage into England (1966)

Trinder B. – The Making of the Industrial Landscape (1982)

Ware M. E. – Narrow Boats at Work (1980)

Wilson E. – The Ellesmere and Llangollen Canal (1976)